Progress Chart

This chart lists all the topics in the book. Once you have completed each page, stick a star in the correct box below.

Page	Topic	Star	Page	Topic	Star	Page	Topic	Star
8	I know the parts of my body	☆	15	I can tell light from heavy	☆	22	I know where the seeds are	☆
9	I can find the eyes	☆	16	I know that all living things grow	☆	23	I know where animals live	☆
10	I know that ears hear sound	☆	17	I know which ones are adults	☆	24	I care about the environment	☆
11	I know what makes the loudest sounds	☆	18	I know that all living things reproduce	☆	25	I know what things are made of	☆
12	I know what smells nice	☆	19	I know that animals use their tongues to taste things	☆	26	I know what a metal is	☆
13	I know what things taste like	☆	20	I know the parts of a plant	☆	27	I know what floats	☆
14	I can say what things feel like	☆	21	I know how seeds grow	☆	28	I can say if it has changed	☆

(!) **When you see this symbol you need to take extra care - ask an adult to supervise you.**

Page	Topic	Star	Page	Topic	Star	Page	Topic	Star
29	I know if it is light or dark	☆	41	I can spot living things	☆	53	I can name the parts of my body	☆
30	I know where the light comes from	☆	42	I know that animals need to eat to live	☆	54	I know that animals use their eyes to see	☆
31	I know which is the brightest light	☆	43	I know that plants are living things	☆	55	I know that I use my nose to smell	☆
32	I know how sounds are made	☆	44	I know the stages of a plant's life cycle	☆	56	I know that animals use their ears to hear	☆
33	I know what makes a shadow bigger	☆	45	I know about herbs, shrubs, and trees	☆	57	I know about senses	☆
34	I know what makes it work	☆	46	I know that some plants make seeds	☆	58	I know what my sense organs do	☆
35	I know pushes and pulls make things move	☆	47	I know about fruits and vegetables	☆	59	I know that some materials are natural	☆
36	I know what mirrors can do	☆	48	I know that all livings things feed	☆	60	I know which types of paper are strong	☆
37	I know what happens	☆	49	I know what to eat to keep my body healthy	☆	61	I know about metals	☆
38	I know that I am alive	☆	50	I know about healthy foods	☆	62	I know how sounds are made	☆
39	I know when something is alive	☆	51	I know that exercise keeps me healthy	☆	63	I know about wood	☆
40	I know about non-living things	☆	52	I know what to eat to keep my teeth healthy	☆	64	I know what happens when you stretch elastic bands	☆

Page	Topic	Star	Page	Topic	Star	Page	Topic	Star
65	I know about stretching	☆	77	I know what things move by themselves	☆	89	I know which cooled the quickest	☆
66	I know what bent the most	☆	78	I know that there are different animal groups	☆	90	I know that some changes can be reversed	☆
67	I know that some things squash, bend, or stretch	☆	79	I know that forces can make things speed up	☆	91	I know which changes are reversible	☆
68	I can tell rough from smooth	☆	80	I know which things can move in water	☆	92	I know how to make a circuit	☆
69	I know that metals are shiny	☆	81	I know about metals, wood, and plastic	☆	93	I know which moves the fastest	☆
70	I know about living things	☆	82	I know how to find out which material is best for a job	☆	94	I know that things move in different ways	☆
71	I know how animals can be grouped	☆	83	I know that you can see through some materials	☆	95	I know that a hard push makes things move quickly	☆
72	I can find what sort of living thing it is	☆	84	I know how to find out which material is best for a job	☆	96	I know that forces start and stop things	☆
73	I know how animals are suited to their habitat	☆	85	I know which materials will keep me dry	☆	97	I know that forces can make things change direction	☆
74	I know that different animals live in different places	☆	86	I know that some things float	☆	98	I know about wall sockets and batteries	☆
75	I know the stages of a life cycle	☆	87	I know that some things melt when they are hot	☆	99	I know that electricity can be dangerous	☆
76	I know about feathers, shells, and hair	☆	88	I know that some things change when they are cooled	☆			

Once you have completed this book, you've earned the certificate overleaf!

Certificate

Grades
K-2

Congratulations to

....(Name)

for successfully
finishing this book.

Well done!

Age..................Date...................

Science

Science made Easy

Kindergarten – Grade 2

Ages **5–8**

Canadian Editor
Marilyn Wilson

DK

EDITOR Julia Roles
PROJECT EDITORS Ian Whitelaw, Ankush Saikia
DTP CO-ORDINATOR Pankaj Sharma
DTP DESIGNERS Harish Aggarwal, Pushpak Tyagi
PRODUCTION Erica Rosen

First Canadian Edition, 2007

Dorling Kindersley is represented in Canada by Tourmaline Editions Inc.,
662 King Street West, Suite 304, Toronto, Ontario M5V 1M7

ISBN: 978-1-55363-079-1

Colour reproduction by Colourscan
Printed and bound in China by L. Rex Printing Co., Ltd.
07 08 09 10 6 5 4 3 2 1

Discover more at
www.dk.com

An Invitation to *Science made Easy*

Learning science is a major component of the knowledge base needed to live and work in today's world. There is an old adage, "I hear and I forget; I see and I remember; I do and I understand." *Doing* is the basis of inquiry science, which uses a constructivist approach to learning, whereby knowledge is constructed from the experiences of the learner. The caveat here is that these experiences must both minimize and address misconceptions about the natural world. For example, we do not catch a cold from the cold, but from a virus. And heavier objects do not fall faster! All objects will fall at the same exact rate if there is no air resistance.

The three workbooks in this series stress an inquiry approach to learning the key ideas in science, while developing the skills needed to do this science. They support how science should be taught as described in the Pan-Canadian Science Curriculum and the Provincial Ministry of Education Science Curriculum Guidelines, and are meant to provide additional support to the learning of science whether at home or at school.

There are three learning levels for *Science made Easy*:

- Grades K–2
- Grades 3–4
- Grades 5–6

On every work sheet, the relevant grade is indicated in a star at the top.

Each lesson in these workbooks has the following sections:

- *Background information:* A key idea in science is described and new science terms are explained.

- *Science activity:* These are all guided activities to explore science and develop the skills for doing science.

- *Science investigation:* These inquiry investigations are learner directed. They provide the learner with the opportunity to elaborate upon or extend a key idea in science. **Investigations involving chemicals, electricity, sharp tools, human subjects, or an open flame must be monitored by an adult. Look for the safety icon (!) shown here for these types of investigations.**

Two support templates follow the worksheets:

- *Science word power:* This worksheet should be used to help the child better understand scientific concepts while building vocabulary.
- *Inquiry template:* The young investigator should use this as a guide for carrying out the *science investigation* described on each page.

At the end of the book you will find the:

- *Answer Section with Notes for Adults:* This section provides answers and explanatory notes for the science activities and investigations.

Where is your nose?
Where are your toes?

Background information
Your body is made up of lots of parts. You have a head, a body (or trunk), two arms, and two legs. Each of these parts is made up of other smaller parts, such as your nose and toes.

Science activity
Use these words to name the different parts of the body.
Write the words on the lines.

head arm leg trunk knee toe elbow
hand nose

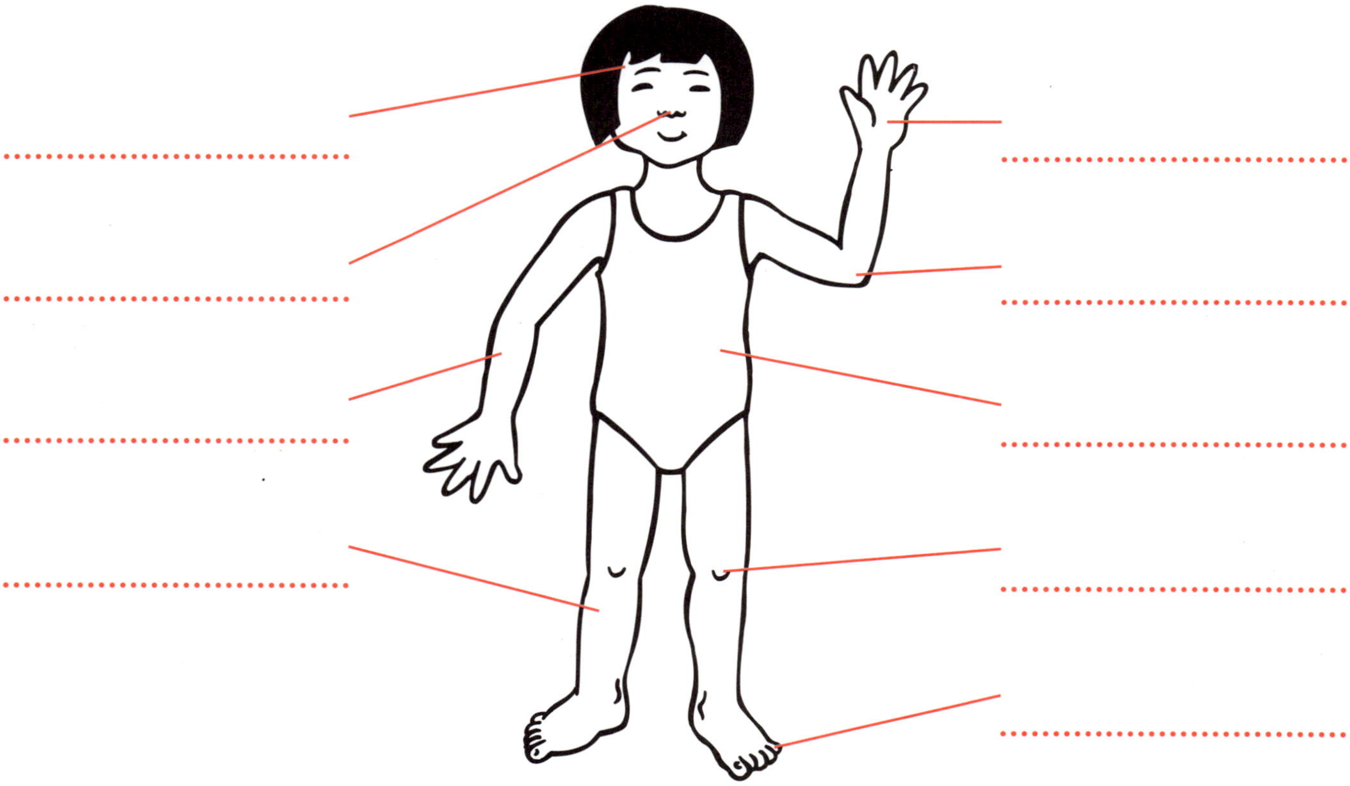

Science investigation

Draw a face with hair, eyes, nose, ears, cheeks, mouth, and a chin.

Can you find the eyes?

Background information

Many animals have eyes. They use them to see. Some eyes are in funny places. Some animals have no eyes at all!

Science activity

Do all these animals have eyes? Find their eyes and circle them.

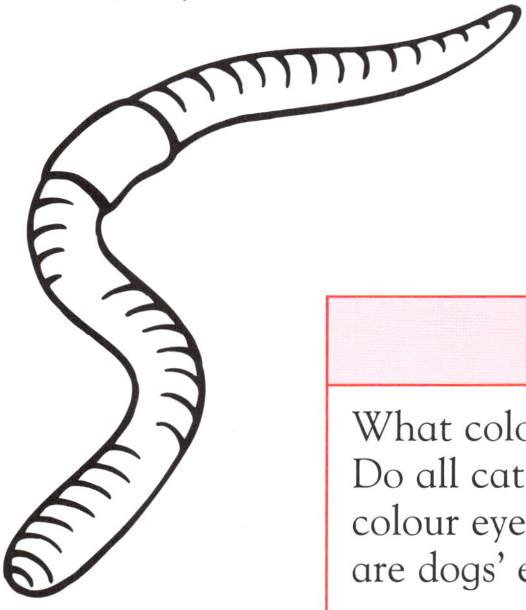

Science investigation

What colour are cats' eyes? Do all cats have the same colour eyes? What colour are dogs' eyes?

What can you hear?

Background information
You use your ears to listen. Lots of different things make sounds. Sometimes you can hear very quiet sounds. Sometimes you can hear very noisy sounds.

Science activity
Find the things in this picture that make a sound.
Draw a line from each one to the girl's ear.

Science investigation

Make a string telephone.
Listen for sounds through your telephone.

How does sound vary?

Background information

You use your ears to hear sounds. Some sounds are loud and easy to hear. Other sounds are quiet and hard to hear. Some sounds are so loud they hurt your ears. People can wear ear protectors to protect their hearing in places where sounds are very loud.

Science activity

If you stood next to each of these things, which one would sound the loudest? Place a check mark (✔) on the box beside it. Which one would sound the quietest? Put an (✘) in the box beside it. Circle the one that is so loud you would need to wear ear protectors to stand near it.

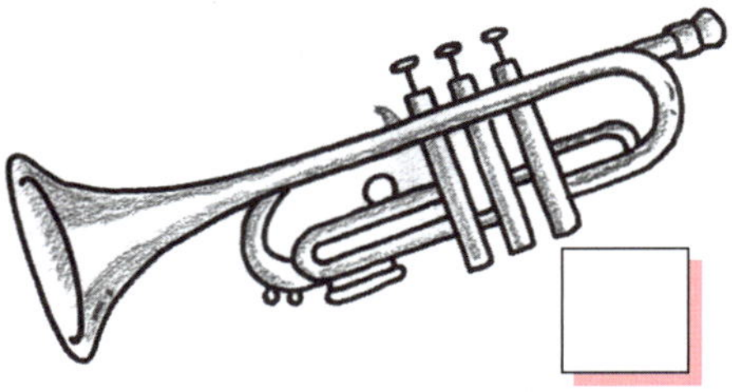

Science investigation

Place some popcorn on a wooden cutting board. What happens when you tap harder and harder with a wooden spoon?

Does it smell nice?

Background information
Some smells are nice, some are nasty. Everybody has favourite smells. Which smells do you like?

Science activity
Which of these smells do you think are nice, and which ones do you think are nasty? Draw a ☺ if it is nice and ☹ if it is not.

perfume

vinegar

cheese

curry

garbage can

bread

car exhaust

Science investigation

(!) What does it look like inside your nose? Use a small flashlight and mirror to find out – but never put anything up your nose!

What tastes best?

Background information

You use your tongue to taste things. Some things taste sweet, some taste salty. Some things taste sour and others taste bitter.

Science activity

How do these things taste? Draw a line from each picture to the word that matches its taste.

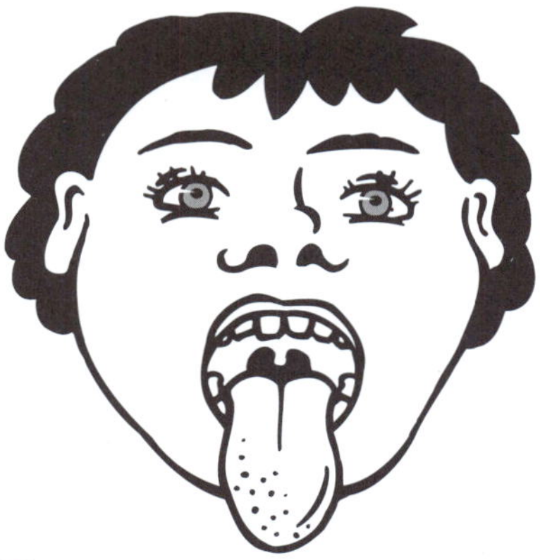

orange peel

sucker

salt

water

lemon

bitter	salty	sweet	sour	no taste

Science investigation

Can you tell the difference between salty, sour, and sweet things if you close your eyes and hold your nose when you taste them? With an adult, investigate with different foods.

What does it feel like?

Background information

You touch things with your fingers to find out what they feel like. You can also feel things with other parts of your body, such as your elbows or your toes.

Science activity

What would you feel if you touched each of these things?

holly leaf

feather

pin

water

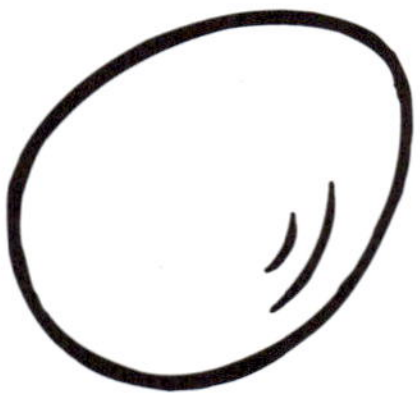

egg

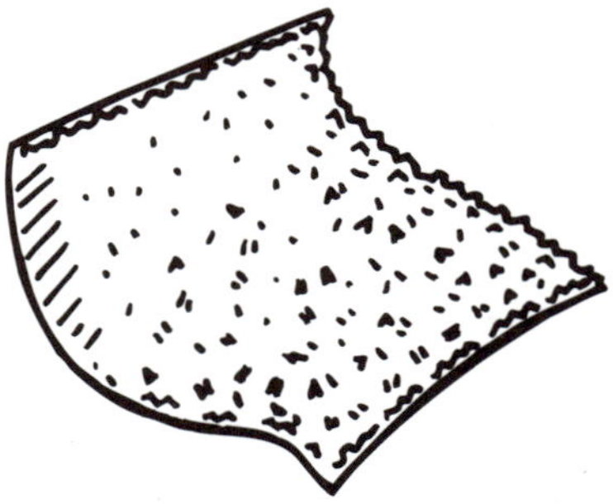

sandpaper

wood

hair gel

Science investigation

(!) Close your eyes and see if you can tell what something is just by the way it feels.

Is it light or heavy?

K

Background information

You can use your hands to feel if something is light or if it is heavy. Heavy things are more difficult to carry. Some things are so heavy that you need a crane to lift them.

Science activity

Draw a ring around each light thing.

Which thing is the lightest? Which is the heaviest?

Science investigation

Find something that is as heavy as a bag of sugar.

K

Do all living things grow?

Background information

Are you growing bigger? All living things grow. When you eat, your body uses some of the food to help you grow.

Science activity

Place a check mark (✔) in the box beside each picture that shows a living thing growing bigger.

Science investigation

Have an adult measure your height at least once a week. Are you growing? Explain. Keep track of your height. Record the date each time it is measured.

Do you look like your parents?

Background information

All animals can make more of themselves. They do this by *reproducing* themselves. Male and female animals are needed to produce the young or *offspring*. Young animals eat and grow into adult animals.

Science activity

Draw lines to connect the male, female, and young in each family.

Science investigation

Some adults look very different from when they were young. Learn about growing frogs using resource books or the Internet.

Do all living things reproduce?

Background information

Have you ever seen a puppy? Puppies are the babies of dogs. Dogs and all living things make more of themselves by *reproducing*.

Science activity

Draw a line joining each parent to its baby. The first one is done for you.

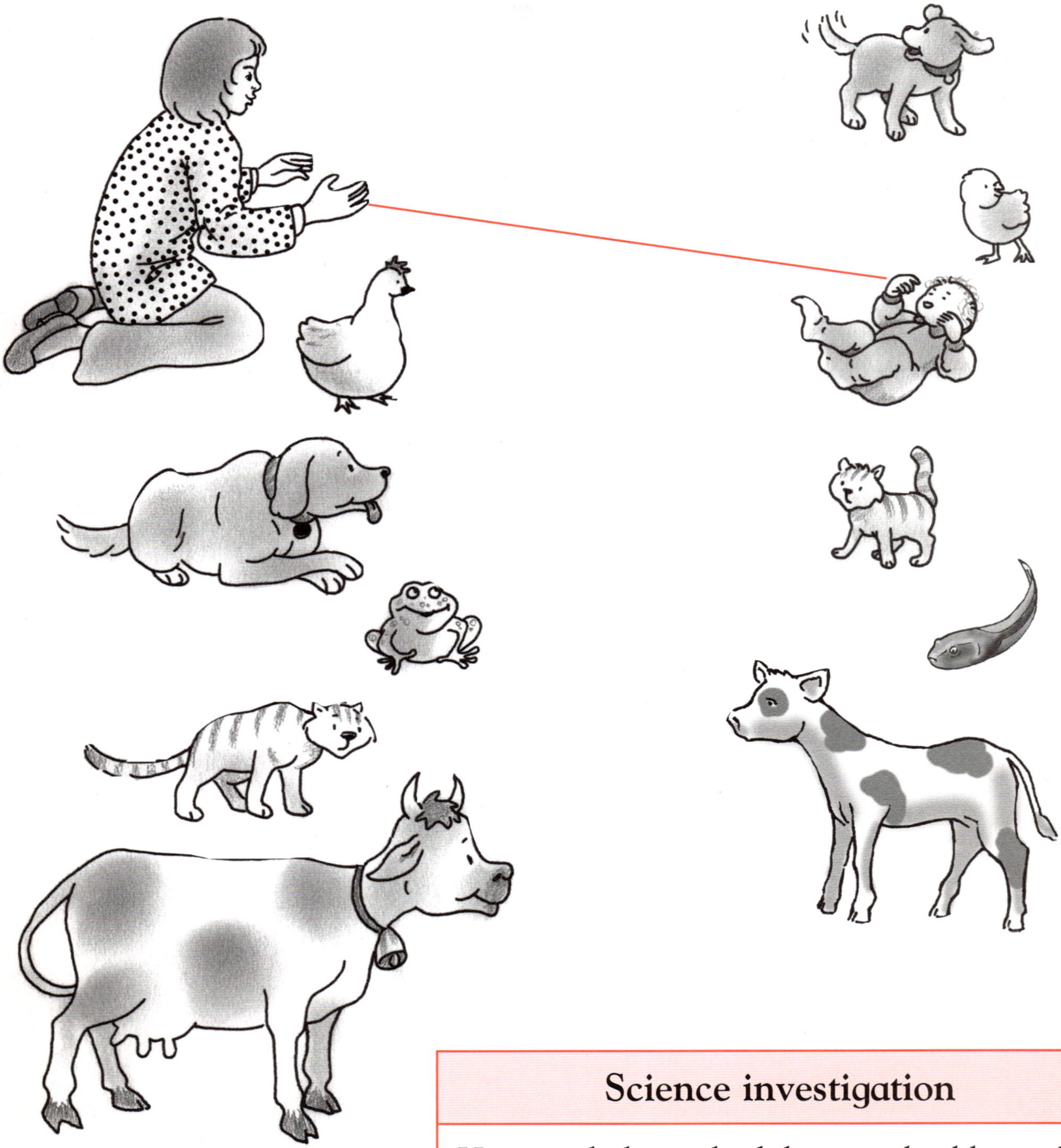

Science investigation

How are baby and adult animals alike and different? Show this in a scrapbook.

What does it taste like?

Background information

Many living things taste their food with their tongues. Some animals twist their tongues to smell food

Science activity

Draw an (✘) on the tongues of these living things.
What does each one like to eat?

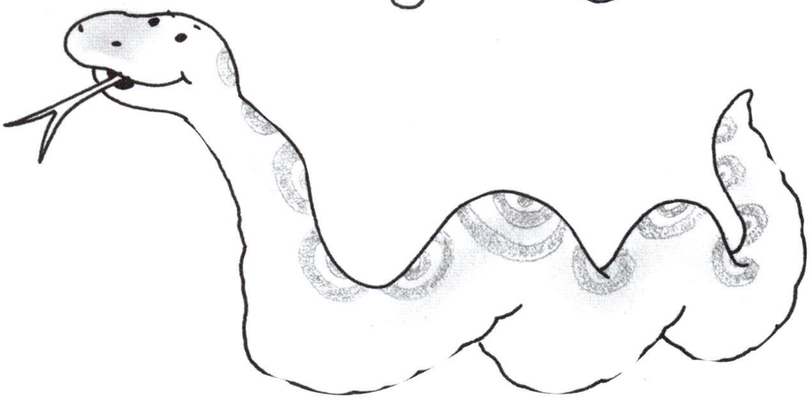

Science investigation

(!) Close your eyes, hold your nose, and taste various foods. Can you tell them apart? Try again without holding your nose.

K

What body parts does a plant have?

Background information
A plant has a body, which is called a stem. Instead of arms and legs, it has leaves and roots. Many plants have flowers as well.

Science activity
Be a plant detective and name the parts of the plant from the clues. Draw a line from each clue to the right word.

Clues	Words
This part is often very colourful.	stem
This part is green and flat.	root
This part is below the ground.	leaf
This part is green, thin and grows upwards.	flower

Science investigation

With an adult, visit a garden, park, or shop.
How many different types of flower can you see?

What makes it grow?

K

Background information

Beans and peas are seeds. To make a seed grow, you must give it water and soil, and you must keep it warm. When it starts to grow, you must keep it in the light.

Science activity

This bean seed was planted a few weeks ago. Can you put the pictures in the correct order to show how the bean grew? Write the letters in the correct order on the line.

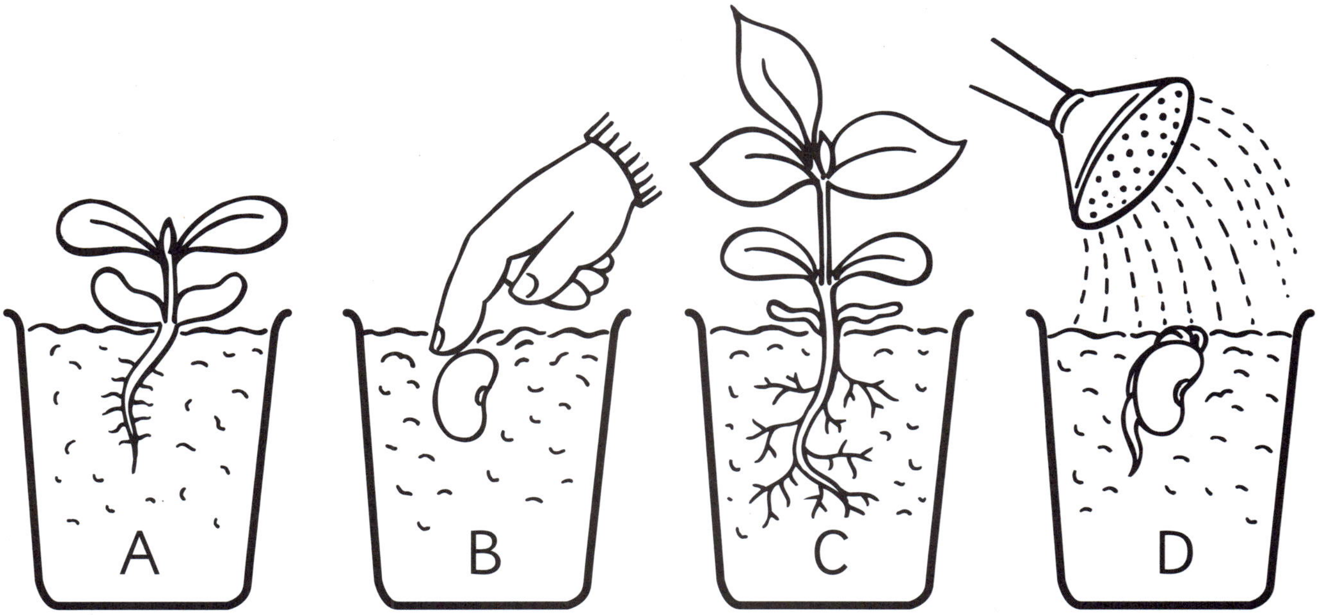

Science investigation

(!) How many different kinds of seeds can you find in a packet of birdseed?

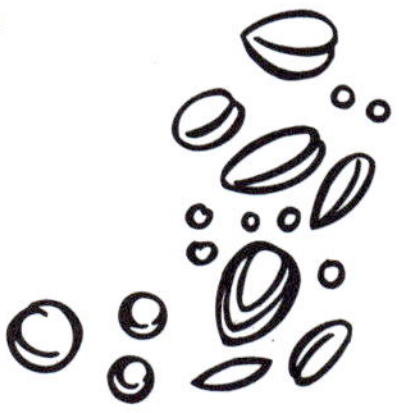

Can you find the seeds?

Background information

If you look inside fruit, you will see that most have seeds.
If you plant a seed and give it water, it will grow into a new plant.

Science activity

Find and colour in the seeds in these fruits.

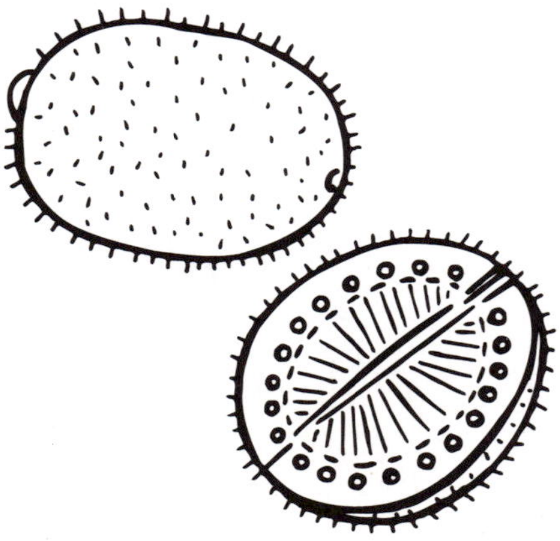

Science investigation

What will happen if you plant the seeds from an orange?

Where does it live?

Background information

Different animals live in different places. Some live in trees, others live in grass, on walls, or under stones and leaves. Some animals live in ponds or the sea. Others live underground.

Science activity

Draw a line from each animal to the place where you would expect to find it.

Science investigation

What sort of animals would you find living in the sea?

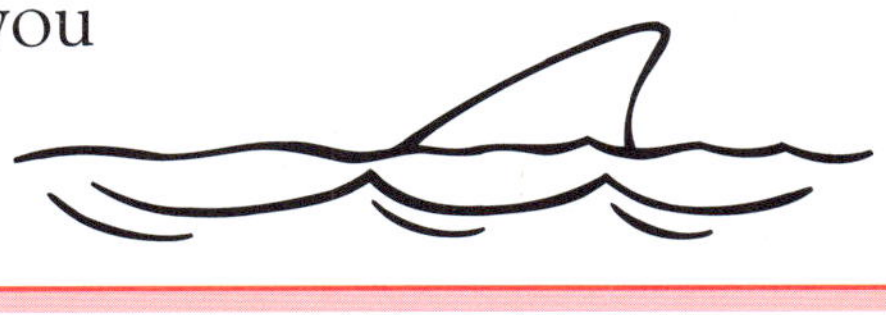

Is it tidy?

K

Background information

When you walk in the park, you sometimes see garbage that people have left behind. This garbage looks horrible and it can harm the animals and plants that live there.

Science activity

Look at this untidy park. Be a litter-detective and find 13 things that people should have put in the garbage can.

Science investigation

Find out where the garbage goes after the truck picks it up. What do you recycle?

What is this material?

Background information
If you look around your house, you will see that different things are made from different materials. These materials include wood, metal, plastic, brick, and glass.

Science activity
What are these things made from? Draw a line from each picture to the right material.

brick

metal

glass

plastic

wood

Science investigation

What things are made from paper in your house? Collect different items. Put them in order from thickest to thinnest.

What is metal like?

Background information

Metal is a very hard material. When you hold metal, it feels cold. If you smell metal, it smells like metal. Metal things look shiny. Metal makes a tinkling sound when you drop it.

Science activity

Colour in the things that are made of metal.

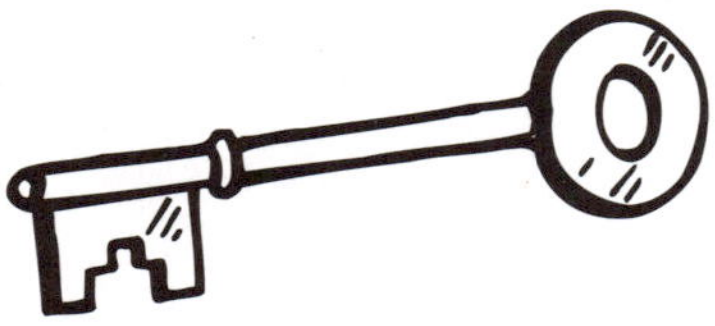

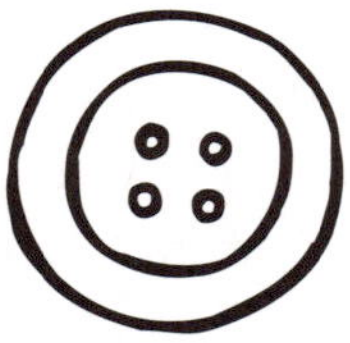

Science investigation

Try holding a magnet near to different metal things. What happens?

Does it float?

K

Background information
Some things float and some things do not. When you put a toy boat in water, it floats on the surface.

Science activity
Have a look at this tank of water. Draw a ring around all the things that float.

Science investigation

Does a sheet of aluminum foil float in water? Does a sponge float in water? Investigate and see if you are right.

Does it change?

Background information

If you put water into a freezer, it will change into hard ice.
If you leave a popsicle in your mouth, it changes from hard ice to runny water.

Science activity

Choose and tick ✓ the correct answer to each of these questions.

What happens when you put water in the fridge?

It gets cold. ☐
It gets warm. ☐
It goes hard. ☐

What happens when you shake a bottle of sauce?

It changes colour. ☐
It does not pour. ☐
It pours easily. ☐

What happens when you put cake mixture in the oven?

It goes lumpy. ☐
It goes hard. ☐
It goes runny. ☐

What happens when you put water in a freezer?

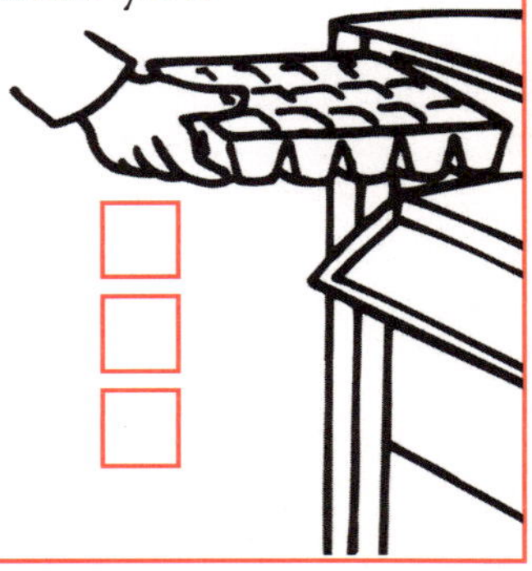

It goes cloudy. ☐
It tastes sweeter. ☐
It goes hard. ☐

What happens when you hold chocolate in your hand?

It melts. ☐
It goes hard. ☐
It tastes better. ☐

Science investigation

What changes happen when you make a Jell-O?

Is it light or is it dark?

K

Background information

When the Sun shines, it is light. At night, it is dark. You can make it light when you switch on a lamp.

Science activity

Will it be light or dark if you do these things? Put a ring around the correct word.

Light a candle in a dark room

Light or dark

Hide underneath your covers

Light or dark

Hide inside a big box

Light or dark

Go right inside a cave

Light or dark

Turn the car headlights on at night

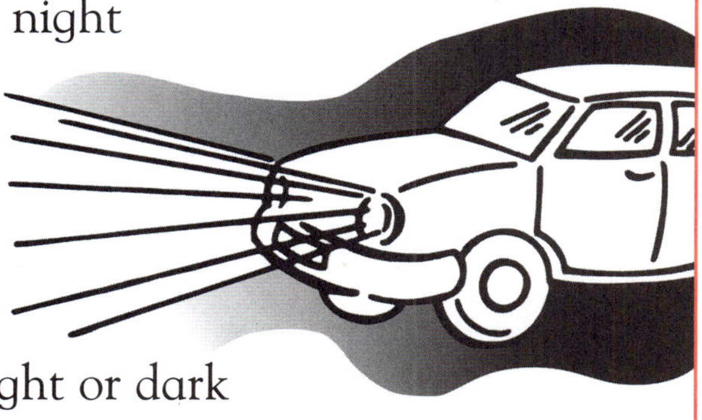

Light or dark

Science investigation

Can you read a book under your covers? What will happen if you use a flashlight?

Where does the light come from?

Background information
It is light in the day because the Sun shines. You can make dark places light by turning on a lamp or a flashlight.

Science activity
Have a look at this picture. Draw a cross X on the things that can make the room light.

Science investigation

Using a battery, some wires, and a bulb, make your own light.

The brightest light

K

Background information

The Sun is a very bright source of light. You must never look directly at the Sun because the bright light can damage your eyes. Light also comes from other sources, which are not so bright. Candles, flashlights, room lights, and table lamps all give out light.

Science activity

Which of these candles gives the brightest light? Write **1** in the box by the brightest light; write **2** in the box by the next brightest; and write **3** in the box by the least bright light.

Science investigation

Draw a picture that shows three light bulbs with different brightness.

What sound does it make?

Background information
You can make *sounds* by plucking, beating, scraping, shaking, or blowing things.

Science activity
Draw a line joining each musical instrument to the word that describes how a sound is made on it.

blow

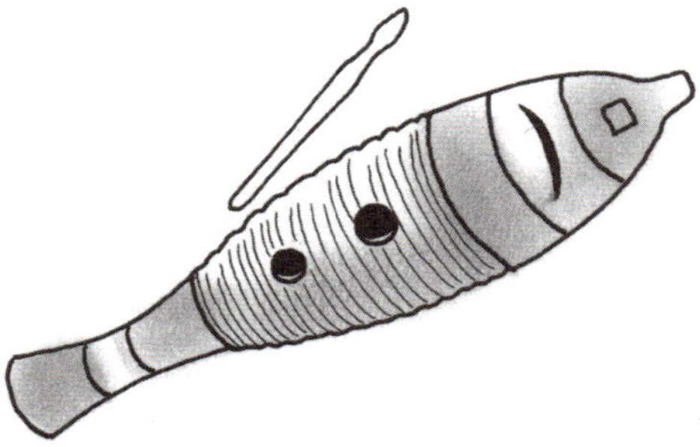

pluck

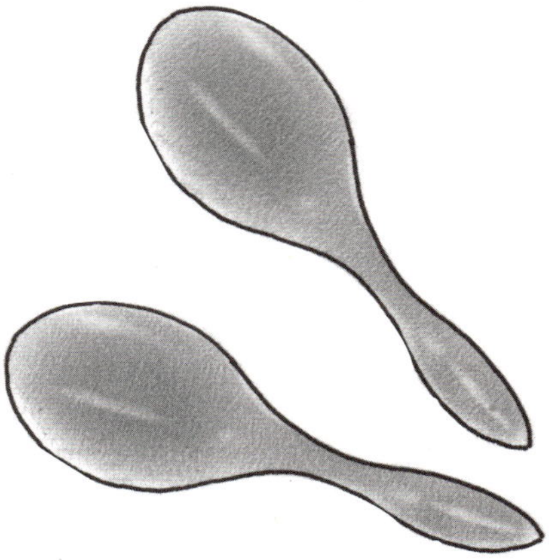

scrape

shake

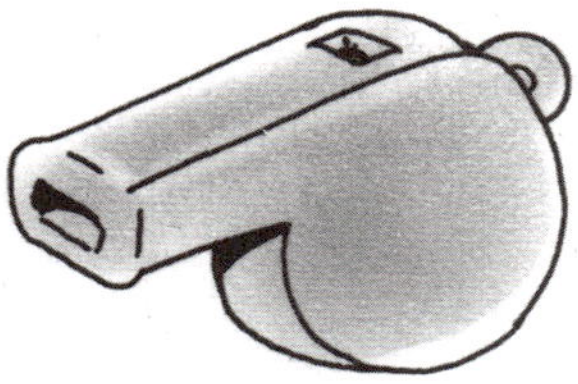

beat

Science investigation

Beat on pieces of wood, metal, and plastic with a wooden spoon. Describe the sounds.

How is a shadow formed?

Background information

When you shine a flashlight at a wall, the wall seems brighter. If you put your hand over the flashlight, it blocks all the light, and the wall stays dark. If you hold your hand between the flashlight and the wall, you make a shadow. The closer your hand is to the flashlight, the bigger the shadow.

Science activity

Which of the children will make the largest shadow? Circle that child's name.

Jo Kate Tom Ben

Science investigation

Use a flashlight and different toys to make shadows on the wall. Make the shadows bigger and smaller.

What makes it work?

Background information
Electricity makes many things work. Some need to be plugged into a socket. Others need batteries.

Science activity
Which things need to be plugged in and which use batteries? Write ✗ for plug and ✓ for batteries.

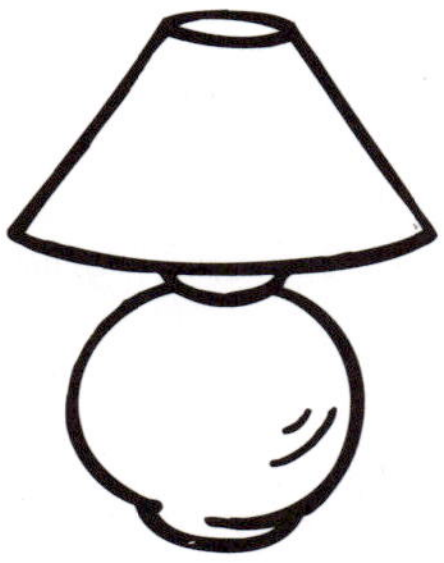

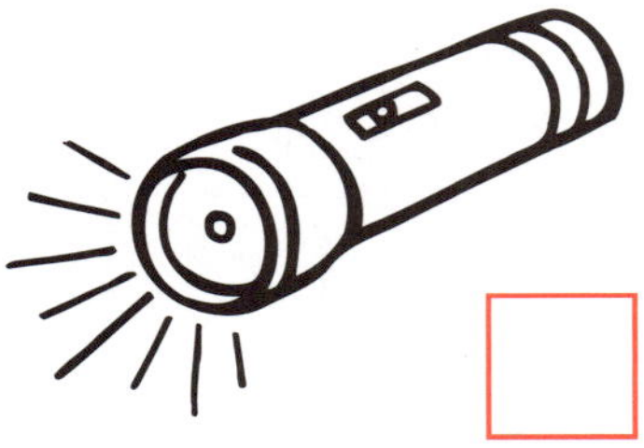

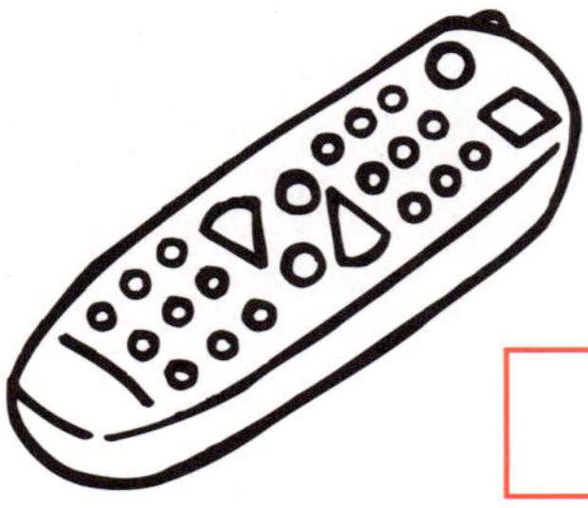

Science investigation

Look inside some things that use batteries. Are all the batteries the same? Draw what you see.

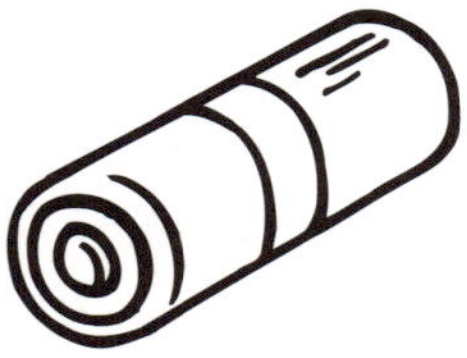

Can we make it move?

Background information

You can make yourself move. You can walk slowly and you can run very fast. You can make other things move when you push or pull them.

Science activity

Think about whether you must push or pull each of these things to make them move. Draw a line to the word push or the word pull.

push

pull

Science investigation

Make a paper plane. Do you push it or pull it to make it work? Try making it go in different directions.

What do I look like?

Background information
When you look into a mirror, you can see yourself. You can also see yourself when you look into other shiny things.

Science activity
Draw what you would see if you looked at yourself in a shiny metal spoon.

The inside of
a large spoon

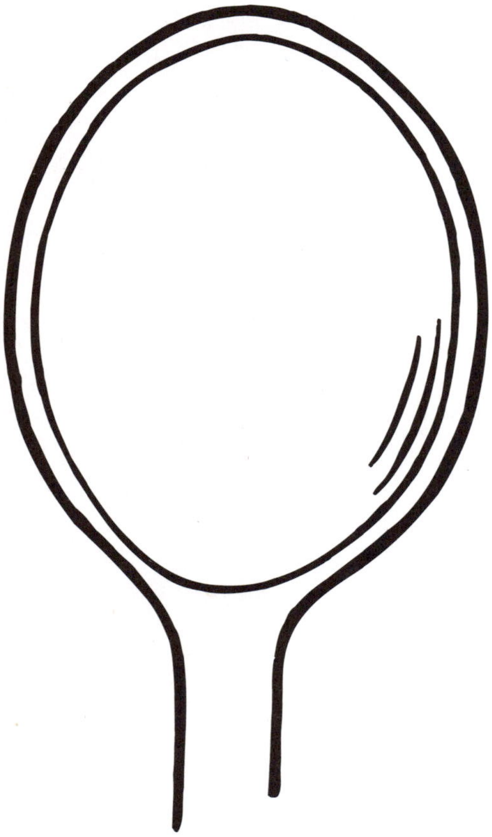

The outside of
a large spoon

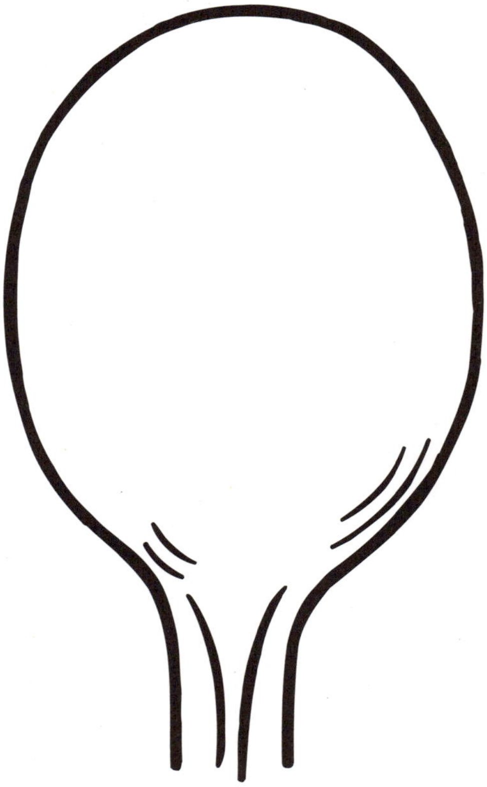

Science investigation

What happens if you close the curtains to make the room dark, and then shine a flashlight at a mirror?

What is happening here?

K

Background information

When you put a marble on a ramp, it rolls down. When you look through clear plastic, things look different. When you look into a mirror, you can see yourself.

Science activity

Try some of these things. What happens?

What happens to a marble rolling down a ramp if you make the ramp steeper?

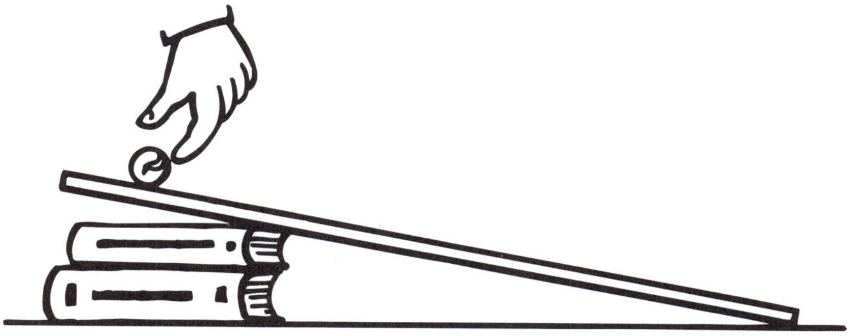

What happens when you look at a blue-coloured object through a red-coloured candy wrapper?

What happens if you look into two mirrors taped together at an angle?

Science investigation

What do you see if you change the angle of the two mirrors?

1

Is it alive?

Background information

You know that things are alive when you see them move by themselves. They can move without being pushed or driven, and they do not need batteries or engines.

Science activity

Draw a circle around each thing that moves by itself.

Science investigation

(!) Can living things move both quickly and slowly? Try to walk slowly and then run. How else can you move? Write a story about how you can move.

Is it a living thing?

1

Background information

Living things can move, eat, and grow. Living things can make more living things. They have babies. Things that are not alive cannot do any of these things.

Science activity

Draw a circle around each living thing that is alive.

Science investigation

Name some living things in your house. Make a list.

1

Was a non-living thing ever alive?

Background information

Living things move, feed, grow, reproduce and react. Living things that can no longer do these things are dead. Some things can never move by themselves, feed, grow, reproduce or react. These things are not alive, and they are called *non-living things*.

Science activity

Draw a circle around each thing that is non-living.

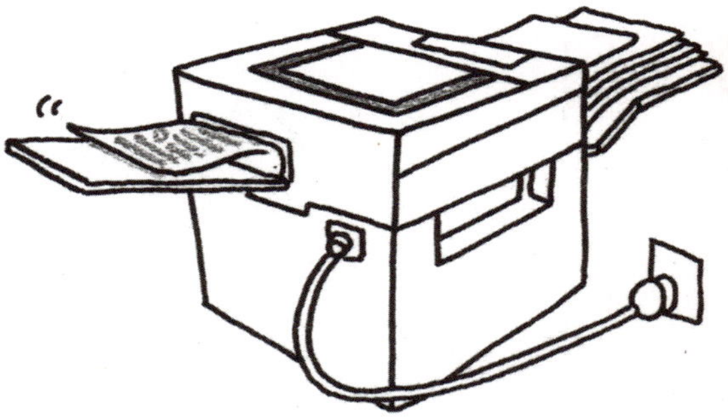

Science investigation

Learn about silk on the Internet. Where does it come from? Is it alive, non-living, or a material that comes from a living thing?

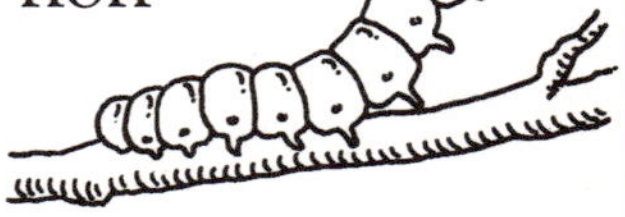

Can you spot the living things?

1

Background information

Animals are living things that can move from place to place by themselves. Animals are living things that eat food and grow bigger. Living things can produce babies.

Science activity

Look carefully at this picture of a farm. Colour in all the things that are alive. Find things that are not alive. Draw a circle around each one.

Science investigation

Cut out pictures or draw pictures of things that are not alive, but were made from living things.

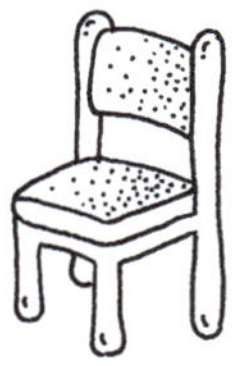

What keeps things alive?

Background information

All animals need to eat food and drink water to stay alive. If animals do not eat or drink, they die. Humans are animals, too, and so need food and water to survive. Some animals eat plants and some eat animals. Humans eat both plants and animals.

Science activity

Draw a line joining each animal on the left to the food it eats.

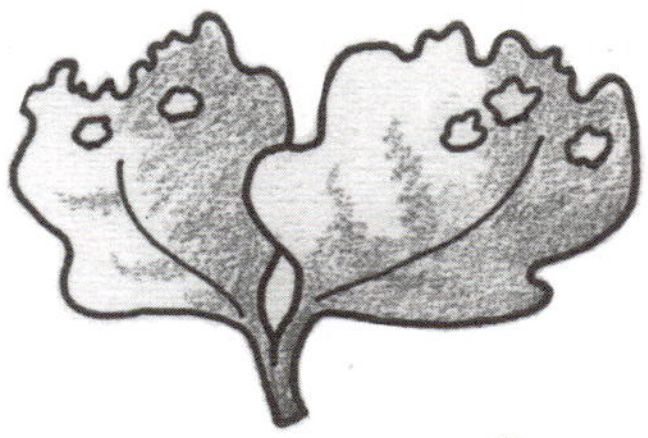

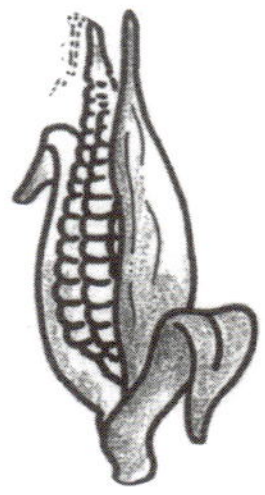
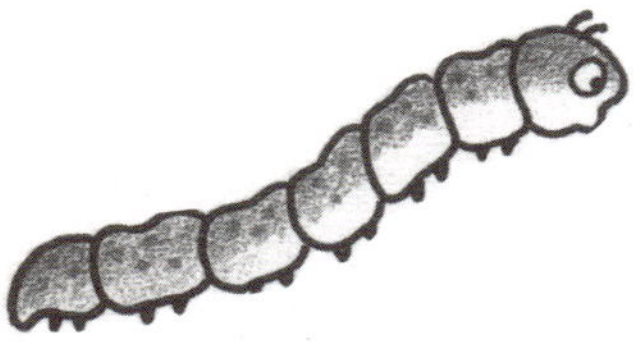

Science investigation

Make a list of all of the foods that you eat. Next to each food, write the name of the plant or animal from which it came.

Are plants living things?

Background information

When we think of living things, we often think of animals. After all, animals move by themselves, grow, feed, react, and reproduce. Although plants do not move from place to place by themselves, they do grow and reproduce. Plants are living things, too.

Science activity

Draw a line joining each whole plant to the part of it that will grow into a new plant.

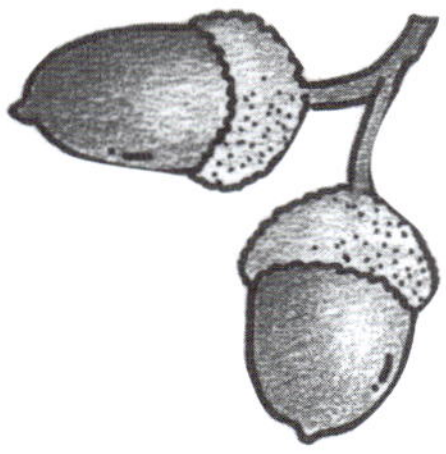

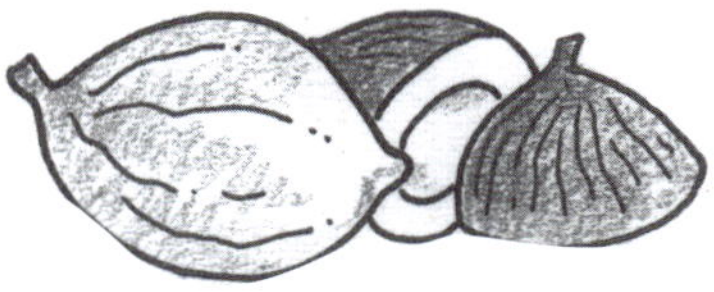

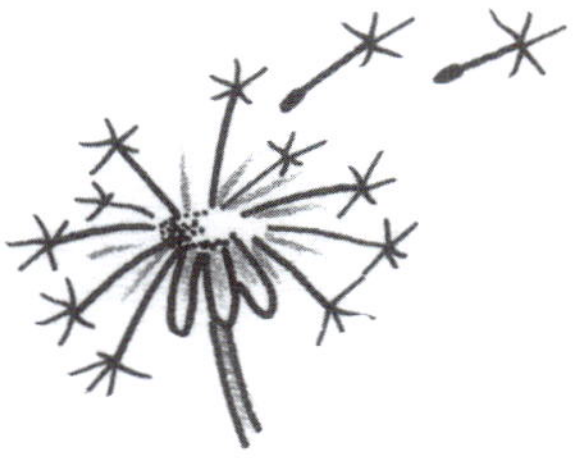

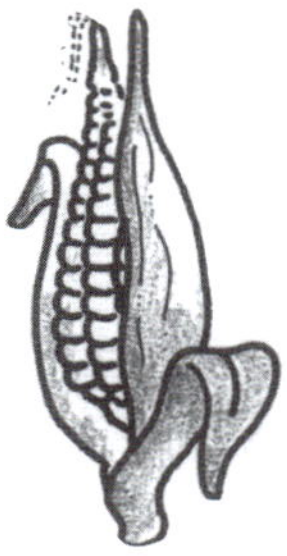

Science investigation

See if you can find an oxalis plant or prayer plant. What happens to its leaves at nighttime? What type of life activity is this? If you do not have a live plant, look in resource books or use the Internet.

1

Do plants have life cycles?

Background information

Many plants produce *flowers*. Flowers make seeds. If a seed lands in soil and gets enough water, it grows into a young plant, called a *seedling*. The seedling grows into an adult plant, which produces flowers. Again, the flower makes seeds that grow into seedlings. These are stages in a plant's life cycle.

Science activity

Here is the life cycle of a dandelion. Which picture goes with which stage in the life cycle? Write **A**, **B**, or **C** in each box.

A

B

C

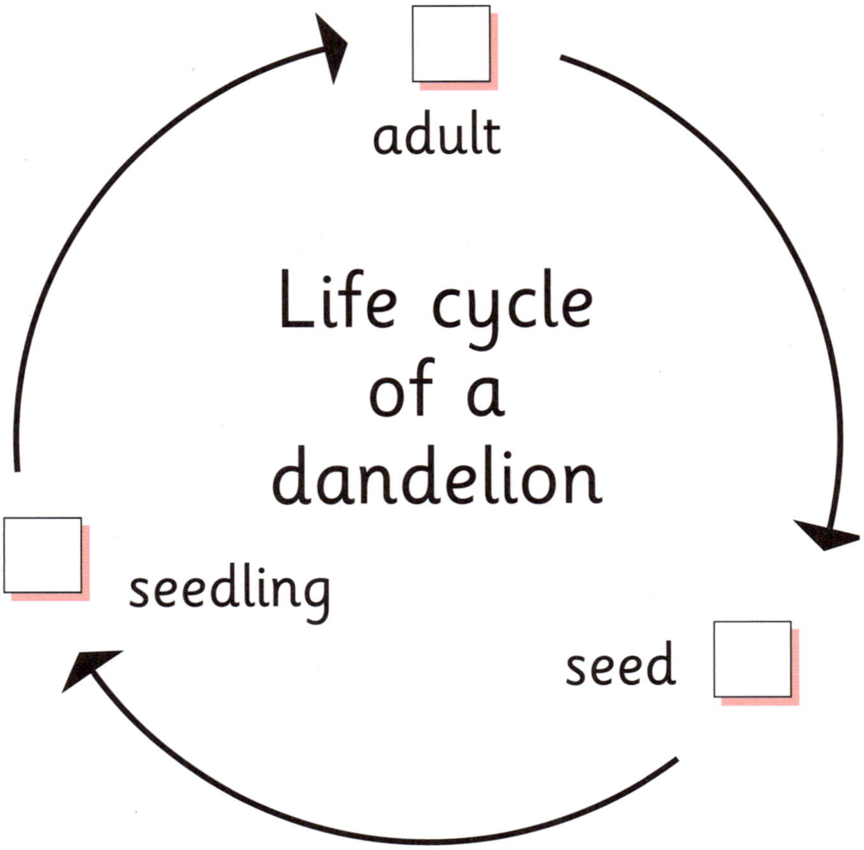

Science investigation

Draw and label the life cycle of a pumpkin.

Are all plants the same?

Background information

There are many different types of plants. *Trees* have a woody trunk and grow very big. Some trees produce seeds in flowers while others produce seeds in cones. *Shrubs* are plants that have more than one trunk and often have flowers. Some plants are small with soft stems. They may have brightly coloured flowers; scientists call these plants *herbs*.

Science activity

Which of the plants below are herbs, which are shrubs, and which are trees? Draw a line from each plant to the correct name. What do all the plants have in common?

herb

shrub

tree

Science investigation

Take a walk in your neighbourhood. Are there more shrubs, herbs, or trees? Draw a picture of your neighbourhood.

Where are the seeds?

Background information

Many plants produce flowers. Part of the flower becomes a fruit. Many types of fruit are good to eat. You often find seeds inside fruits. There are many types of seeds. When seeds are planted, they grow into new plants.

Science activity

These fruits have been cut in half. Find the seeds, and colour them in.

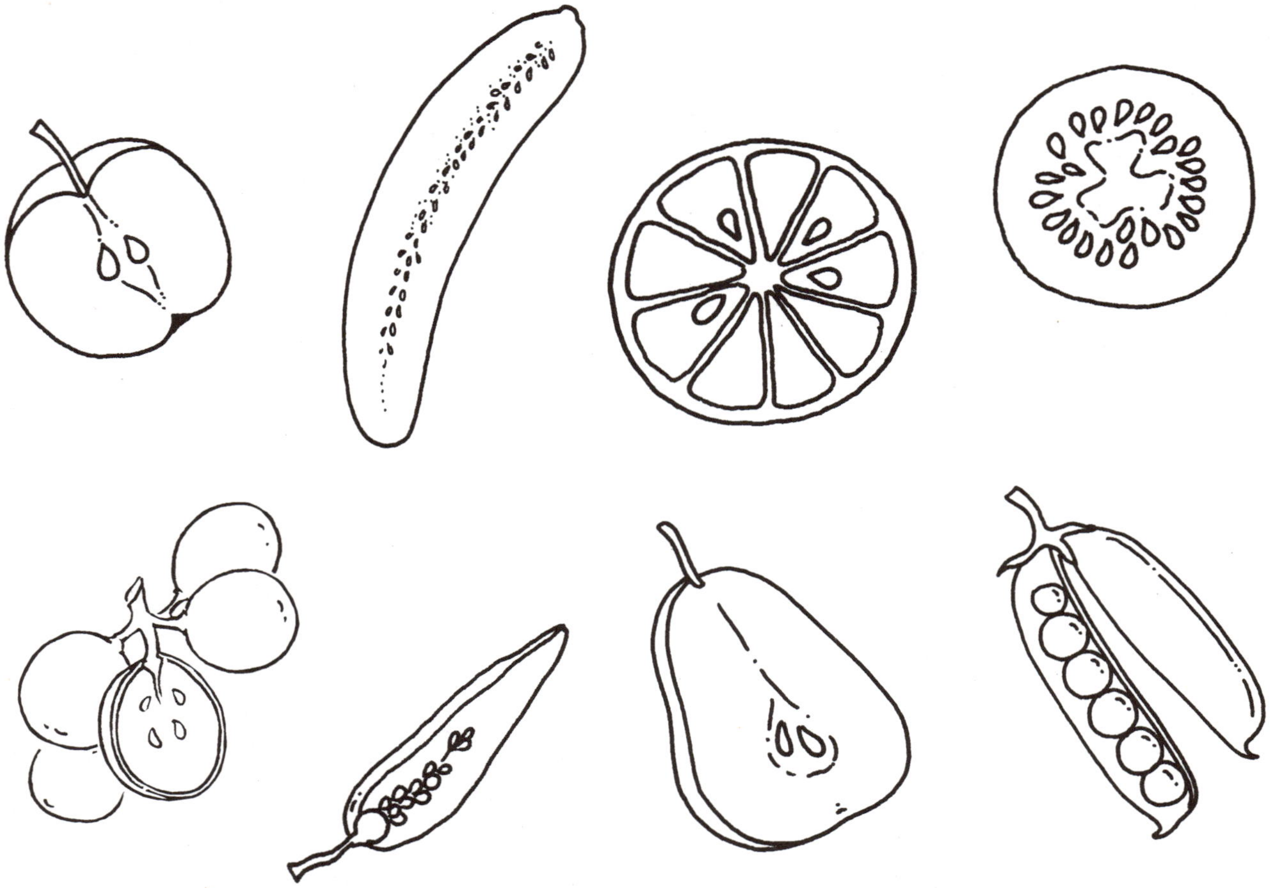

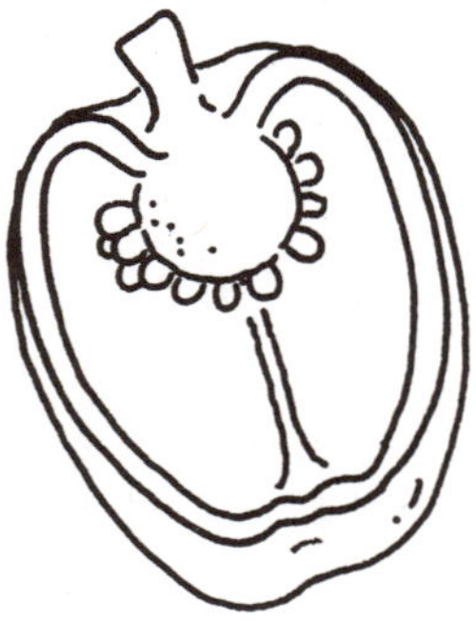

Science investigation

(!) Bean seeds grow inside of a bean pod. Soak 2–3 bean seeds overnight. Plant them in some potting soil. Draw what you see each day.

What kind of plant is it?

Background information

Fruits and *vegetables* are plants that we eat. Fruits are made by flowers. Seeds are made by fruits. Seeds can be found inside of the fruit. Most vegetables are the leaves, stems, or roots of a plant.

Science activity

Sort these foods into vegetables and fruits. Write **F** for a fruit and **V** for a vegetable in the box beside each one.

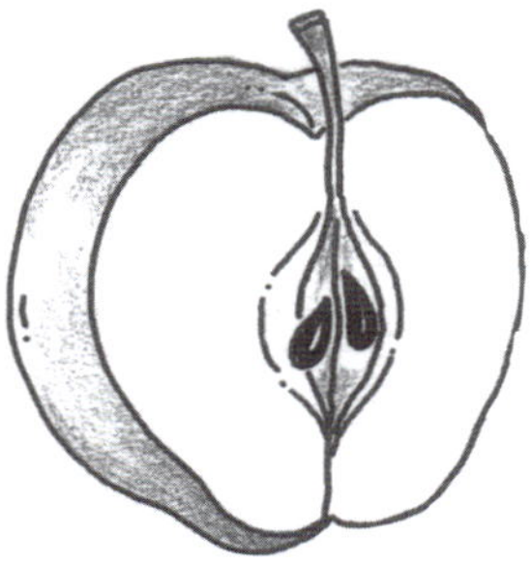

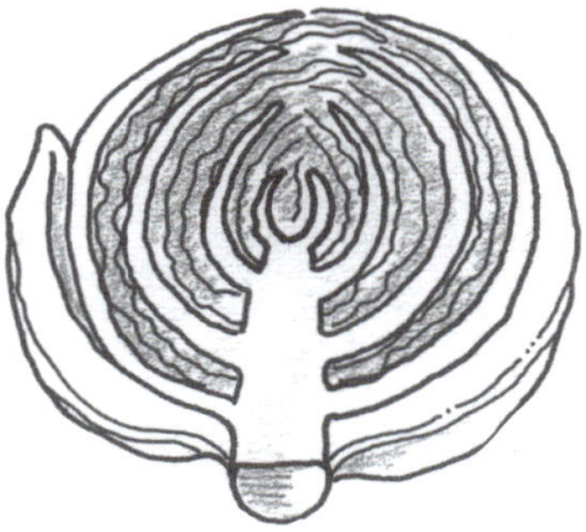

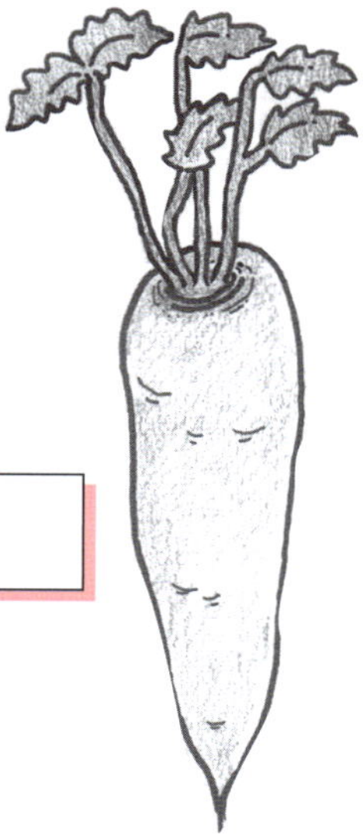

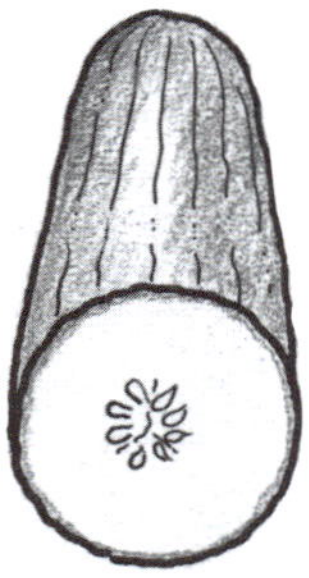

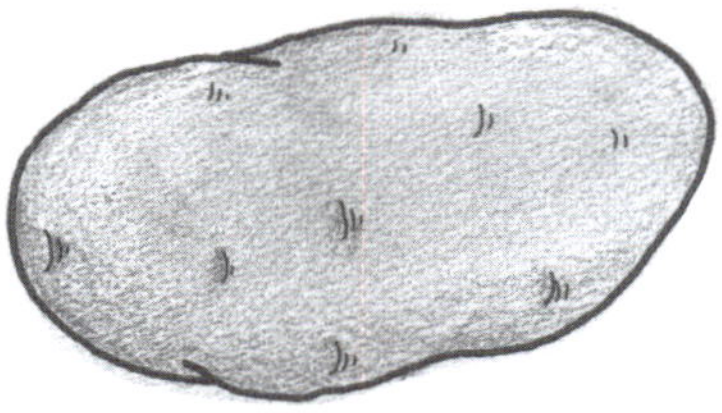

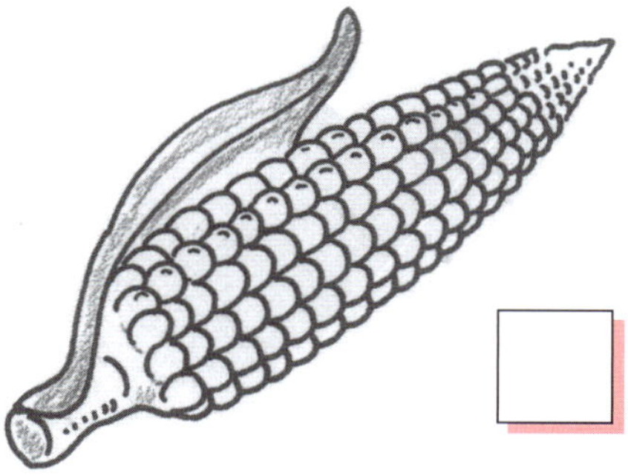

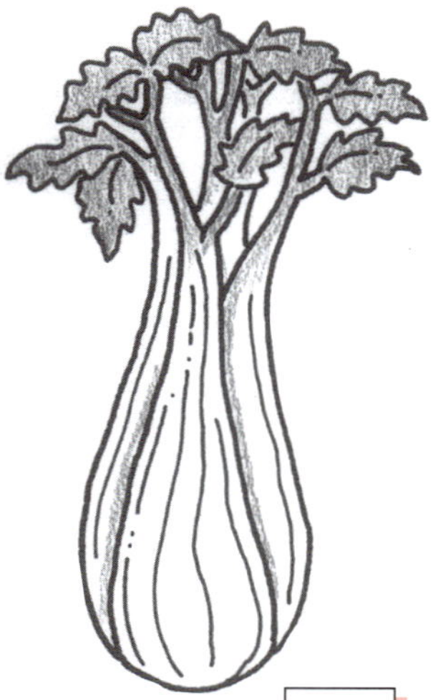

Science investigation

Draw and label what you like to put in a salad to eat.

1

Do all living things feed?

Background information

When something eats, it must be alive. Only living things need to eat food, so they can grow and stay healthy.

Science activity

Draw a circle around each living thing that is eating food.

Science investigation

Can you eat food with either hand? Can you drink when you are upside down? Investigate.

What is healthy eating?

1

Background information

Foods such as beans, milk, meat, and fish help you grow. These types of food have a lot of *protein*. Other foods such as pasta, bread, cereal, rice, and potatoes give you energy to work and play. They are mostly *carbohydrates*. Foods such as butter and cheese also give you energy. They are mostly *fats*. Vitamins and minerals, found in fresh fruit and vegetables, are good for you. Eating the right amount of each type of food is very important to staying healthy. Foods high in salt, sugar, and fats can make you ill if eaten frequently.

Science activity

Look at what Gus and Lakeisha are eating. Who is eating the healthy meal? Place an (✗) over the unhealthy meal. Why do you think it is unhealthy?

Science investigation

(!) Cut out pictures of foods that make up a healthy meal. Draw and label what you ate today.

1 Which kind of food is healthy?

Background information
The food that you eat is good for you in different ways. Meat, milk, eggs, and fish all help you to grow. Bread, rice, potatoes, and fruits give you energy to run and play. Vegetables and fruits also help you to stay healthy.

Science activity
Look at this meal, and draw a line joining each type of food to one of the circles below.

Food for growth

Food for energy

Food for health

Science investigation

Do you eat healthy? Keep track of what you eat every day for a week.

How can you keep healthy?

Background information

You are a human. You need food and water to stay alive. You also need exercise, which keeps you fit. When your body is healthy, it can move easily. When you exercise hard, your body sweats. Sweat is mostly water. It helps to keep you cool.

Science activity

Place a check mark (✔) by each activity that can make you sweat a lot.

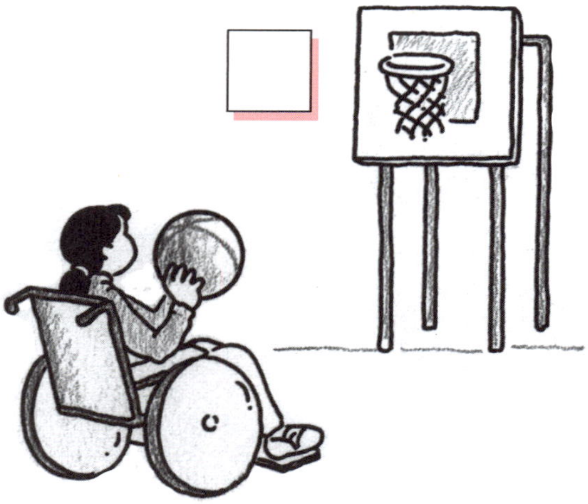

Science investigation

(!) Make a prediction about how exercise will affect your breathing. (1) Count how many breaths you take in 60 seconds. (2) Run in place for one minute. Repeat (1). Were you correct?

How do we keep teeth healthy?

Background information
Some of the things that you eat and drink, such as milk, help to build strong teeth and bones. However, some small bits of food are left on and in-between your teeth when you eat. Sugary foods and drinks can harm your teeth, which may then need to be fixed by a dentist. Fruits and vegetables are healthy snacks because they contain less sugar than cookies and candy. Brushing and flossing your teeth after every meal helps keep them clean. Fluoride from water, vitamins, and toothpaste also help protect your teeth.

Science activity
Which of these foods will help keep you healthy and are better for your teeth? Colour them in.

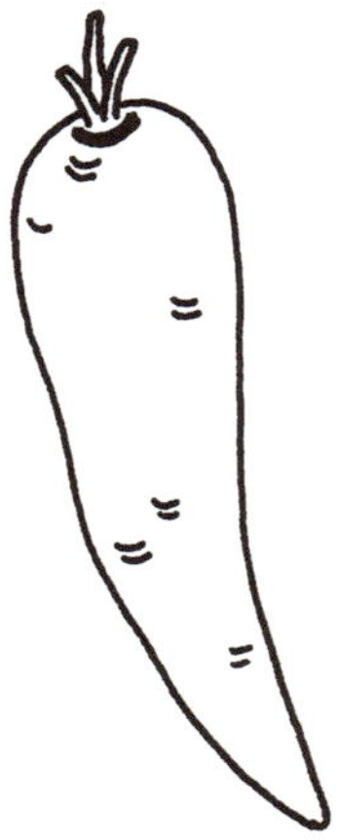

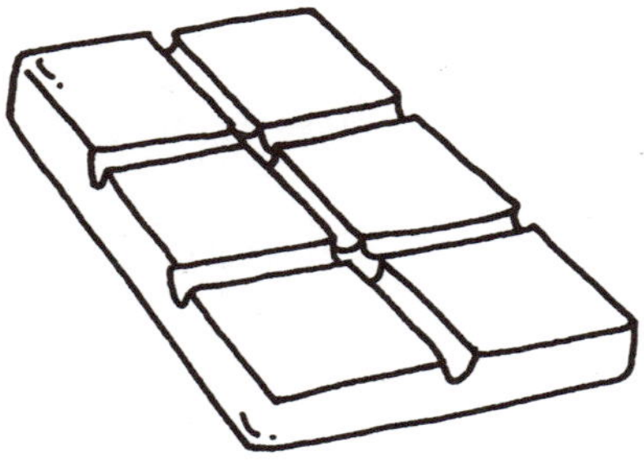

Science investigation

Discuss what you should do to take good care of your teeth.

What are human parts?

Background information
Your body has a head, chest, tummy, legs, feet, arms, and hands.

Science activity
Draw a line from each word below to the correct part of the body.

chest
fingers
head
leg
hand

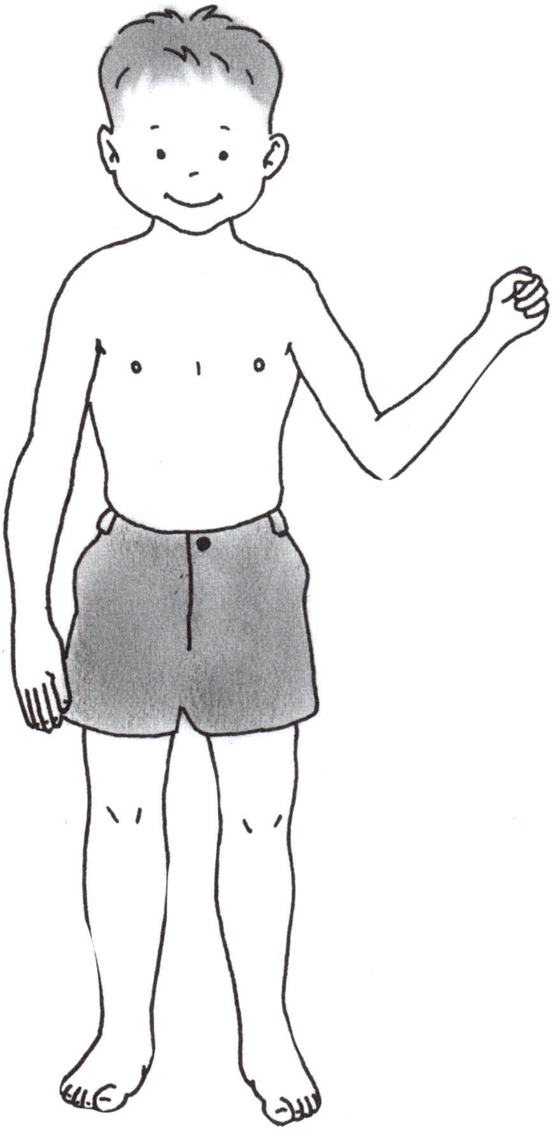

arm
elbow
foot
tummy
toes

Science investigation

Rub an unsharpened pencil on the palm of your hand and then rub it on the knuckle side. Rub the pencil the same way on the top and bottom of your feet. On which side did you feel the pencil more? Record your findings.

Why do we need eyes?

Background information

Many living things have eyes. They use their eyes to see things. Many animals have two eyes.

Science activity

Draw the missing eyes on these living things. Use reference books or the Internet to help you.

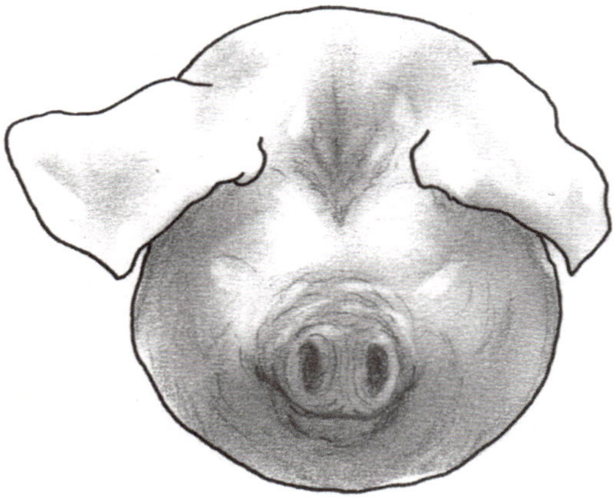

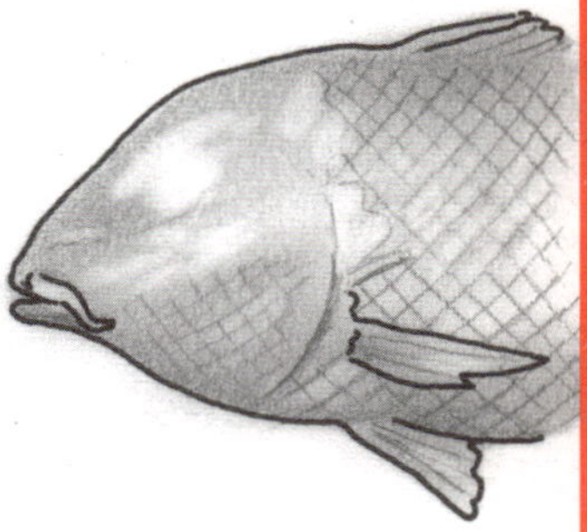

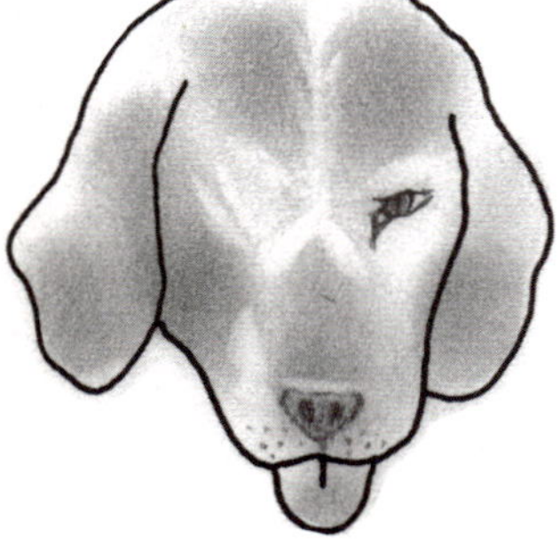

Science investigation

Draw and colour the eyes of your family and friends. How are they alike and different? Find out about the eyes of animals on the Internet.

What are noses for?

Background information

Many living things have noses, which they use to smell things. Dogs have a better sense of smell than humans.

Science activity

Guess which nose belongs to which animal. Follow the wiggly lines to see if you are right.

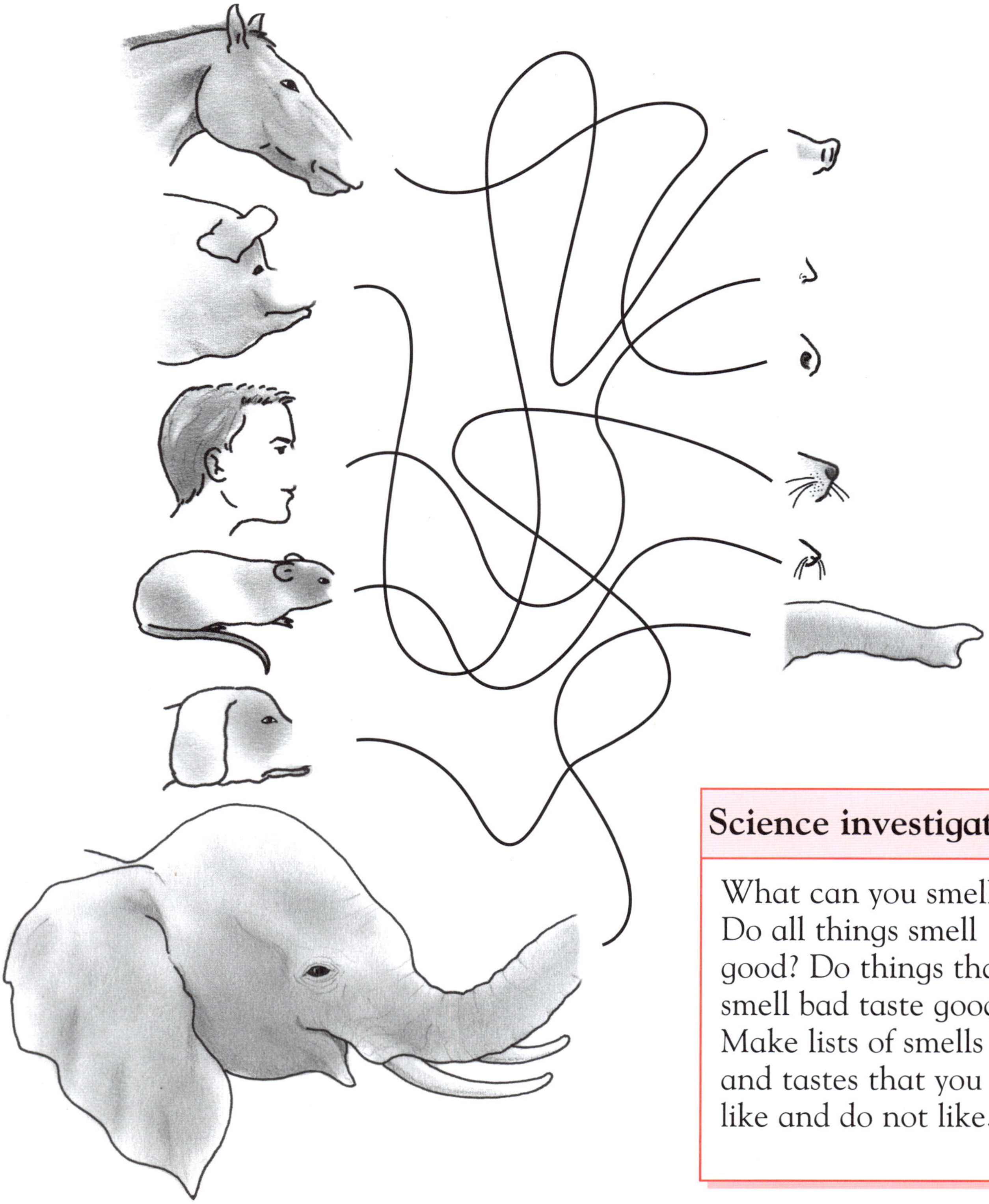

Science investigation

What can you smell? Do all things smell good? Do things that smell bad taste good? Make lists of smells and tastes that you like and do not like.

What do ears do?

Background information

Many living things have ears. They use their ears to hear sounds. Dogs can hear sounds that humans cannot.

Science activity

These animals all have the wrong ears. Draw a line joining each living thing to its correct ears.

Science investigation

What types of sounds are pleasing and not pleasing? Make lists of sounds you like and sounds you don't like.

Which sense is it?

1

Background information

You have senses that tell you what is happening in the world around you. Your senses give you information about sounds, light, smells, tastes, and what things feel like when touched.

Science activity

Different parts of your body sense different things. Choose words from the box below to describe what the boy and the dog in the picture are sensing. Label the parts using each word only once.

sound	light	smell	taste	touch

Science investigation

(!) Can you identify an object with your sense of touch? Place different objects in small paper bags (no sharp objects!). Ask a friend to stick his or her hand in the bag and try to identify what's inside.

1

How aware are you?

Background information

Your body senses and reacts to changes in the world around you. Your ears tell you about sounds; your nose tells you about smells; your tongue tells you about tastes; and your eyes tell you about light. When you touch something, your skin can feel if it is rough or smooth, and hot or cold.

Science activity

How can Sophia sense what is on the table? Draw a line joining each object to the part of her body that can sense it.

Which sense can Sophia not use?

....

Science investigation

(!) Have a friend blindfold you and hand you different objects. How does your sense of touch identify the objects? Did you use any other of your senses?

Is it natural?

1

Background information

Some things come from nature. They are natural. Leather, for example, comes from the skin of a cow and is often used to make shoes. Some things are made from the parts of a plant. Cotton, for example, is used to make cotton shirts. Other things, such as plastics, are made in factories.

Science activity

Draw a line joining each material to the place from which it comes.

wool

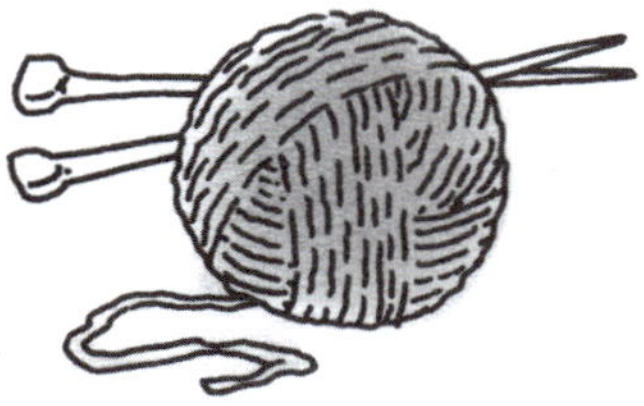

plastic cup

cotton thread

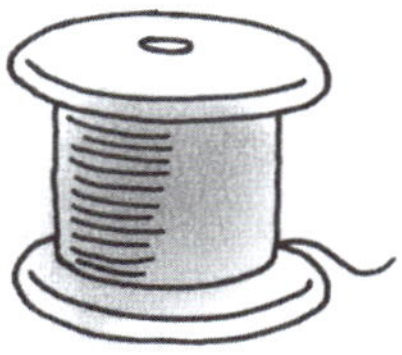

rubber tire

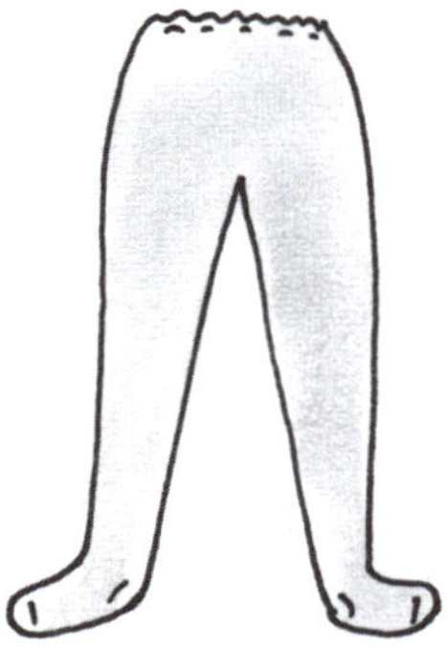

nylon tights

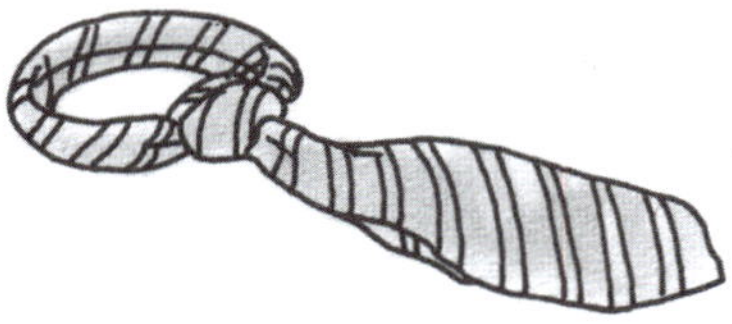

silk tie

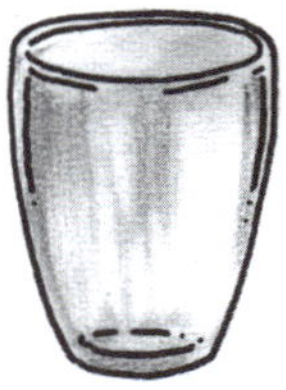

glass

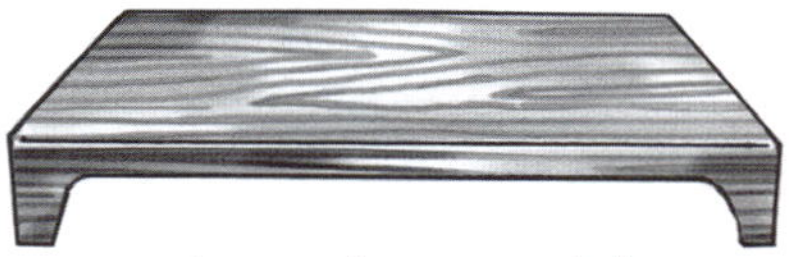

wooden table

Science investigation

Make a chart of natural and factory-made things in your kitchen. Which type of thing is most common there?

1

What is paper made of?

Background information

Paper is made by mixing small pieces of wood with water and chemicals. Paper is used to make books, newspapers, toilet paper, tissue paper, writing paper, wrapping paper, cardboard, paper cups, and many other everyday things.

Science activity

Some types of paper are stronger than others. They can hold other objects without breaking. For example, a paper plate can hold food. Which types of paper below are strong, and which are not strong? Place a check mark (✔) in the correct box in the chart.

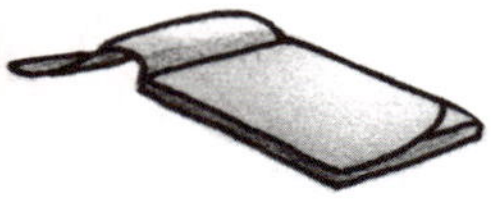

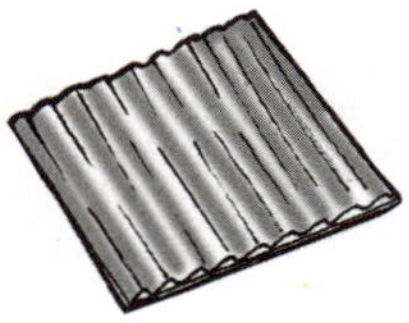

Paper	Strong	Not strong
newspaper		
paper towel		
writing paper		
tissues		
tissue paper		
toilet paper		
cardboard		
paper cup		
wrapping paper		

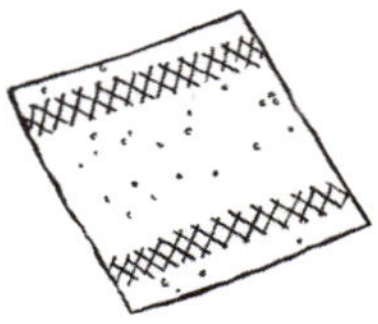

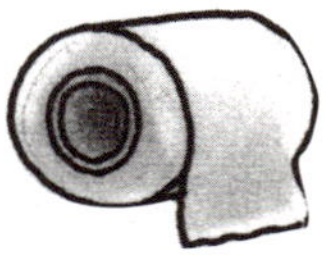

Science investigation

Predict and test which type of paper best wipes up water. Chart what happens.

Is is made of metal?

Background information

Some objects are made of metal. Metal things look shiny. They make a ringing noise when hit. When you touch a metal object, it feels cold. Metals are used to make many things, such as the aluminum foil used to wrap food.

Science activity

Draw a line from each sentence on the left to the metal object on the right that it describes.

This metal tool used for eating feels cold to the touch.

bronze bell

A bag of these sharp pieces of metal used by builders has a strong metal smell.

steel spoon

Its loud metallic sound rings out, catching people's attention.

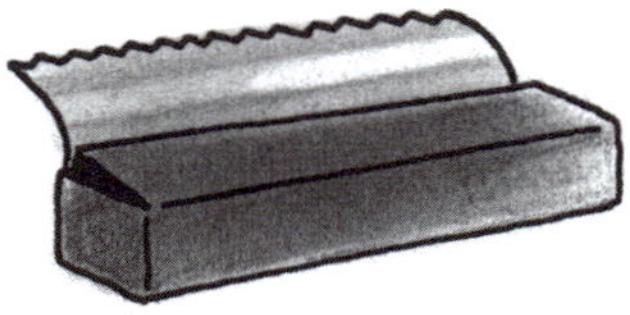

aluminum foil

It is a shiny metal used to wrap food.

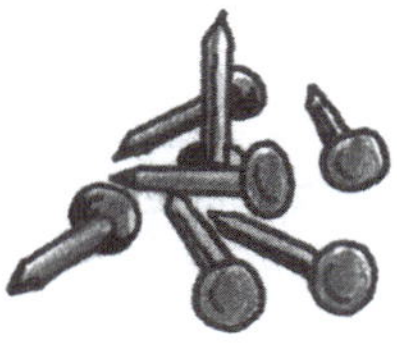

iron nails

Science investigation

Can a magnet pull all metals? Test different metals to see which of them is attracted to a magnet.

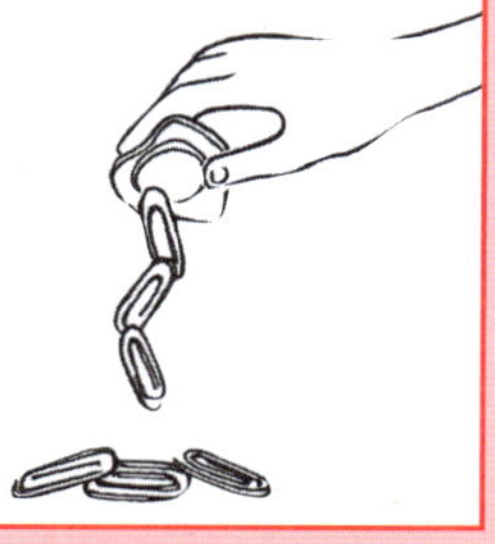

1

How do you make that sound?

Background information

You can make sounds when you beat, shake, or scrape things. You can make sounds when you pluck strings or use a bow. Blowing through a hole can also make a sound.

Science activity

Draw a circle around each instrument that makes a sound when you beat it.

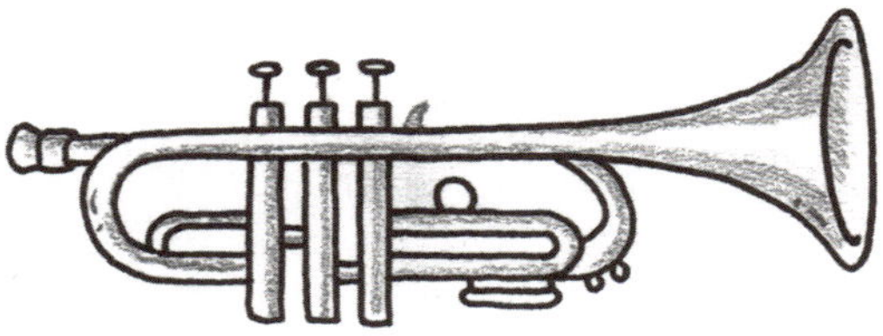

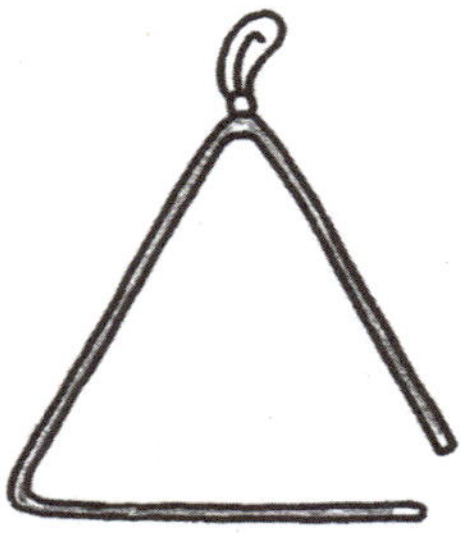

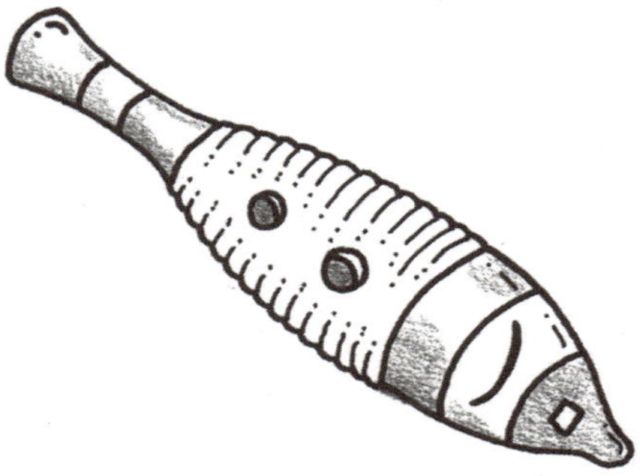

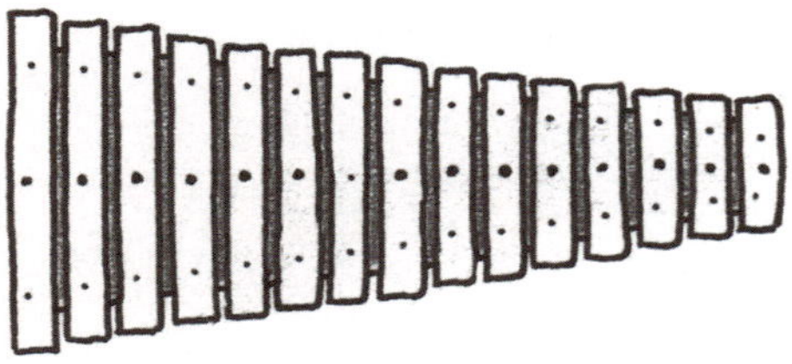

Science investigation

Blow over the neck of a bottle. What happens? Pour a small amount of water in the bottle and blow again. Add more water and repeat. Does the sound change? Explain.

Is it made of wood?

1

Background information

Some things are made of *wood*. Wood comes from trees. Many types of wood can float in water. Unlike metals, wood does not feel cold when touched. Wood can have a special smell, like the wood of cedar.

Science activity

Which things in the chart below are made of wood? Place a check mark (✔) in the correct box in the chart. The first one has been done for you.

Things	Wood	Not wood
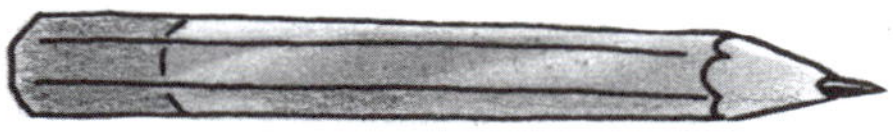	✔	
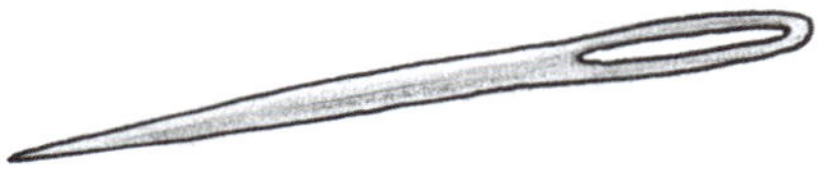		
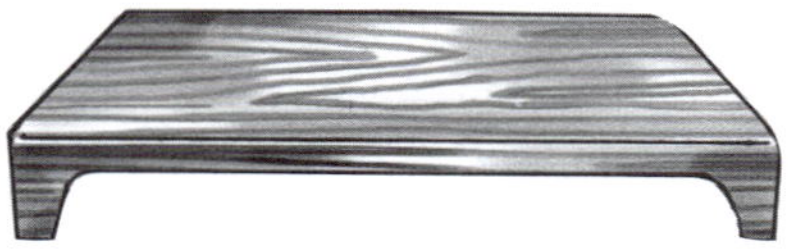		
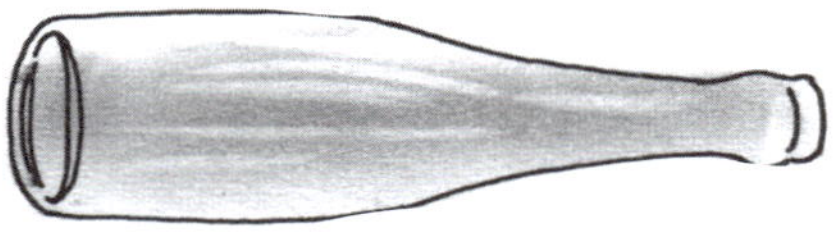		
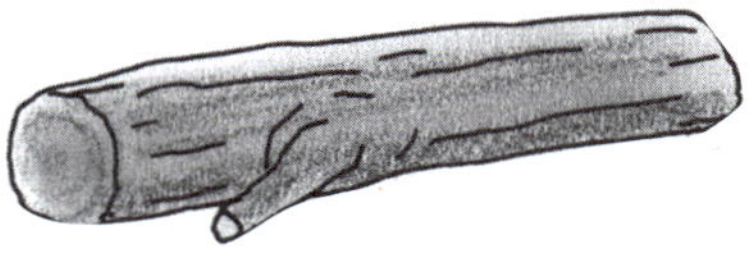		

Science investigation

Place different woods in a large bowl of water. Do they all float?

1

Will it stretch?

Background information

Elastic materials stretch when you pull them. When you stop pulling, they go back to the size they were. Elastic materials also squash when you squeeze them. When you stop squeezing, they go back to their original shape.

Science activity

Annika wanted to find out how elastic bands stretched. She tied three plastic cups to elastic bands and hung the pots from a rail. Then she put three glass marbles into the first pot, four into the second, and five into the third. Here are the results of her experiment.

1 What happens to each elastic band as more marbles are put in the pot below it?

....

2 Draw a fourth pot hanging from the rail. It should show what would happen if six marbles were put into the pot.

Science investigation

Predict what will happen when coins are added to a cup placed on a foam pillow. Test your prediction.

What stretches the most?

1

Background information

Some materials stretch a lot when you pull them. Other materials are hard to stretch.

Science activity

Ella tested pieces of different materials to see how much they stretched. Each piece of material was the same length. She used the same heavy metal to give each material the same amount of pull. She then measured how much each one had stretched. Here are her results. Write **1** in the box under the strip that stretched to the longest length; write **2** under the strip that stretched to the next longest length; and so on.

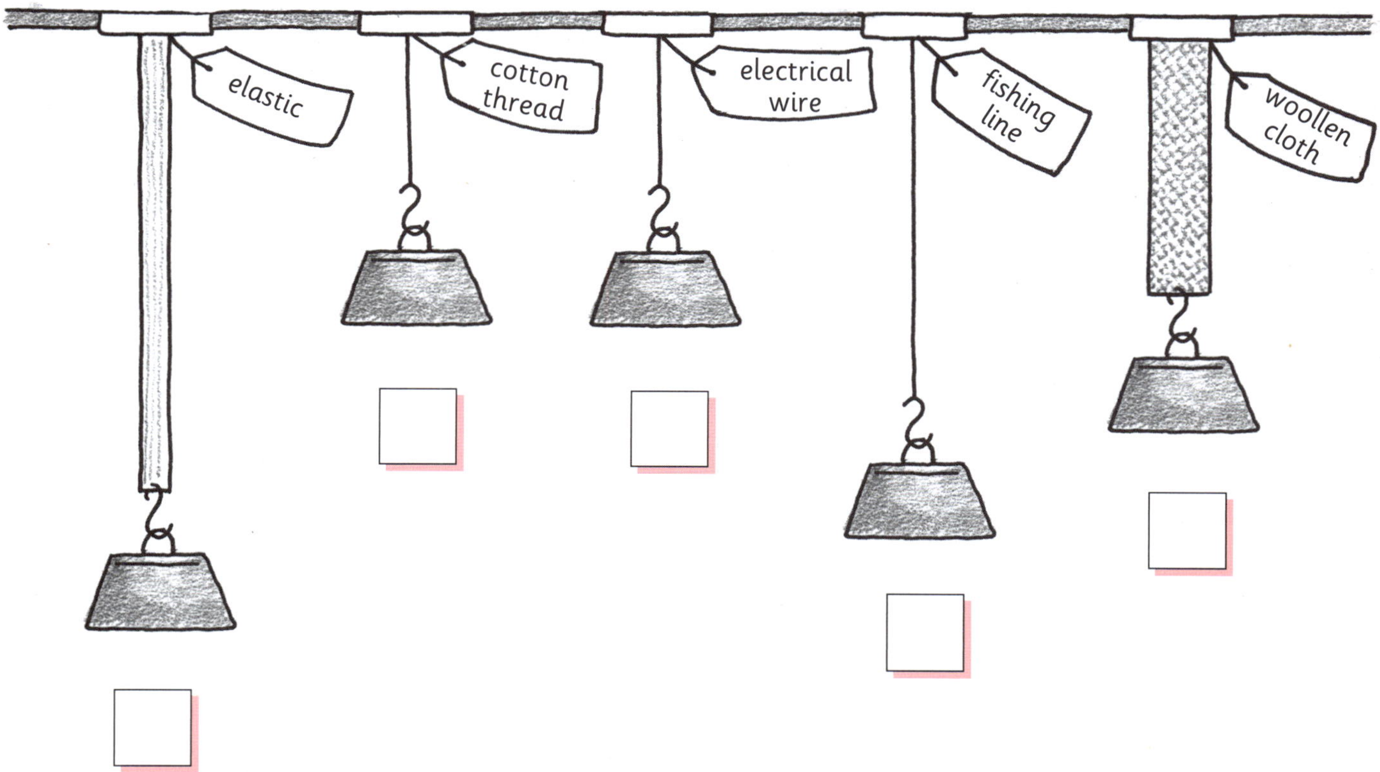

Science investigation

(!) Obtain 3-4 rubber bands of different sizes. Punch a hole near the rim of a small paper cup. Unfold a paper clip to make an "s" shape. Hook one end to the cup and the other end to a rubber band. Holding the rubber band, add pennies to the cup. Measure how much the rubber band stretches. Repeat these steps for each rubber band.

What bends the most?

Background information

Some things, such as plastic bags, bend easily. Other things, such as dinner plates, do not bend at all. The more you push or pull some things, the more they bend. Things that are not bendable may break.

Science activity

Drew is gently squeezing some cups to find out which material is the easiest to bend. Write **easy** below the cup that Drew will find the easiest to bend. Write **hard** below the cup that he will find the hardest to bend.

china

plastic

paper

Science investigation

Try to bend a stack of cards. Now try bending fewer cards. How does the number of cards affect their ability to bend?

Is it squashy, bendy, or stretchy? 1

Background information

Some things you can squash; some things you can bend; some things you can stretch; and some things you can twist. When you let them go, some things go back to their original shape.

Science activity

Colour in all things that you can bend. Place a check mark (✔) by things you can squash. Place a cross (✘) by things that you can stretch, and which then go back to the shape they were before.

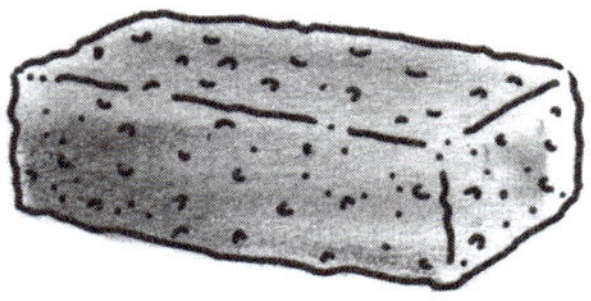

☐ sponge

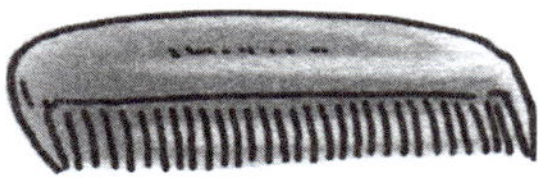

☐ plastic comb

☐ paper ball

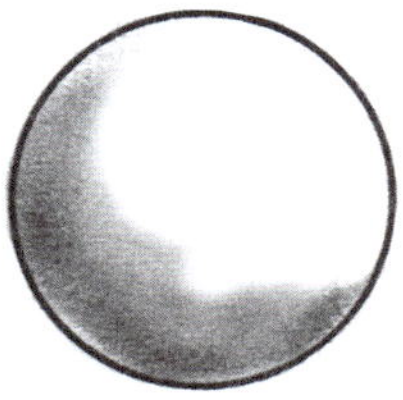

☐ rubber ball

☐ tomato

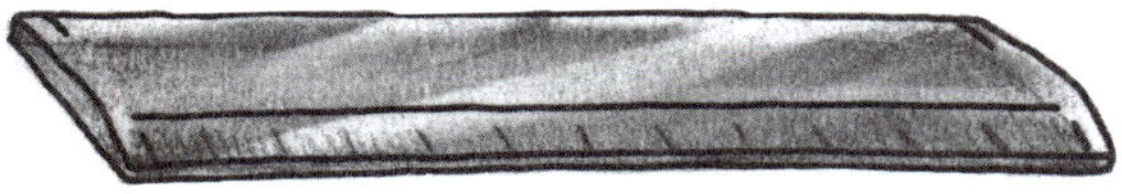

☐ plastic ruler

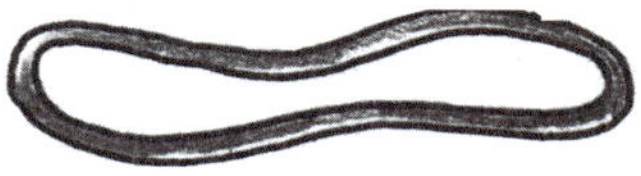

☐ rubber band

☐ newspaper

Science investigation

(!) Describe all the properties of a rubber band. Describe all the properties of clay or plasticene.

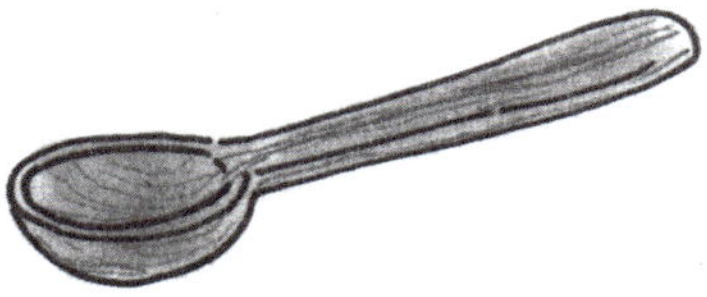

☐ wooden spoon

Is it rough or smooth?

Background information

Some surfaces are smooth. Your hand can slide over them easily. Some surfaces feel rough. They feel bumpy when rubbed. Very rough surfaces can hurt your hand if you rub them.

Science activity

Which of these surfaces is the roughest? Which is the smoothest? Can you list these things in order of roughness? Write the roughest one first.

glass bottle

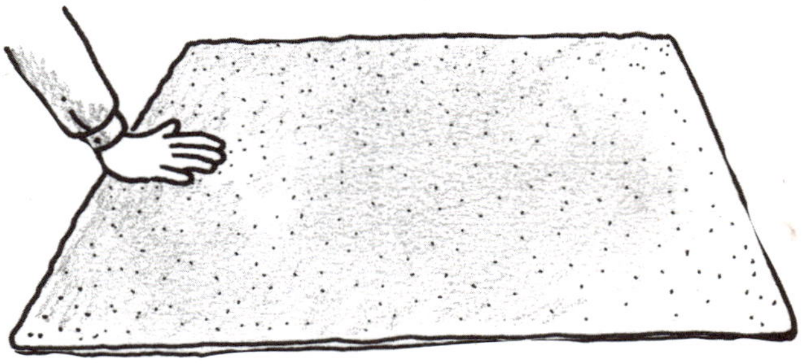

carpet

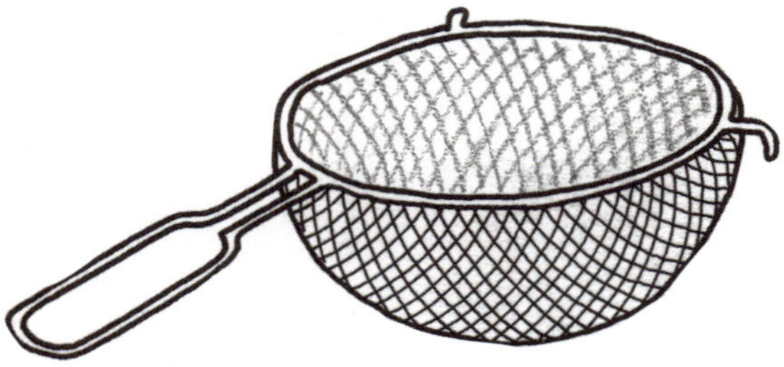

sieve

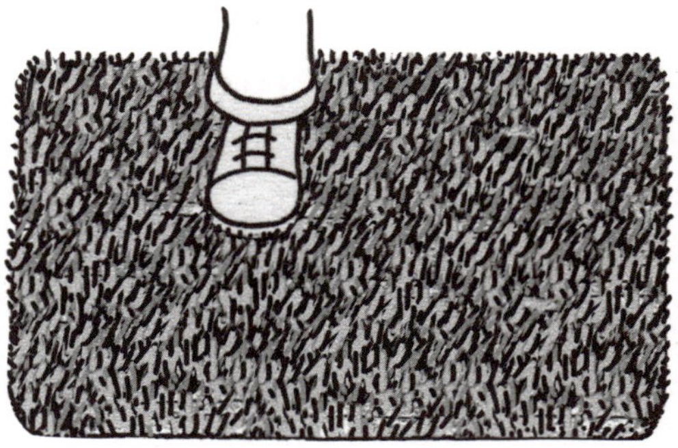

doormat

Science investigation

Find fabrics that feel rough or smooth. List them under each heading–rough and smooth.

1 ....

2 ....

3 ....

4 ....

Is it shiny?

Background information

Metals are often shiny. If the surface of a metal is polished, you can see your reflection when you look at it. This is why metals are used to make mirrors. If you shine a flashlight onto a shiny metal surface, you can see a reflection of the light on the wall.

Science activity

Which of these spoons is made of metal? Place a check mark (✔) in the correct box.

Which of these spoons is the shiniest? Place a check mark (✔) in the correct box.

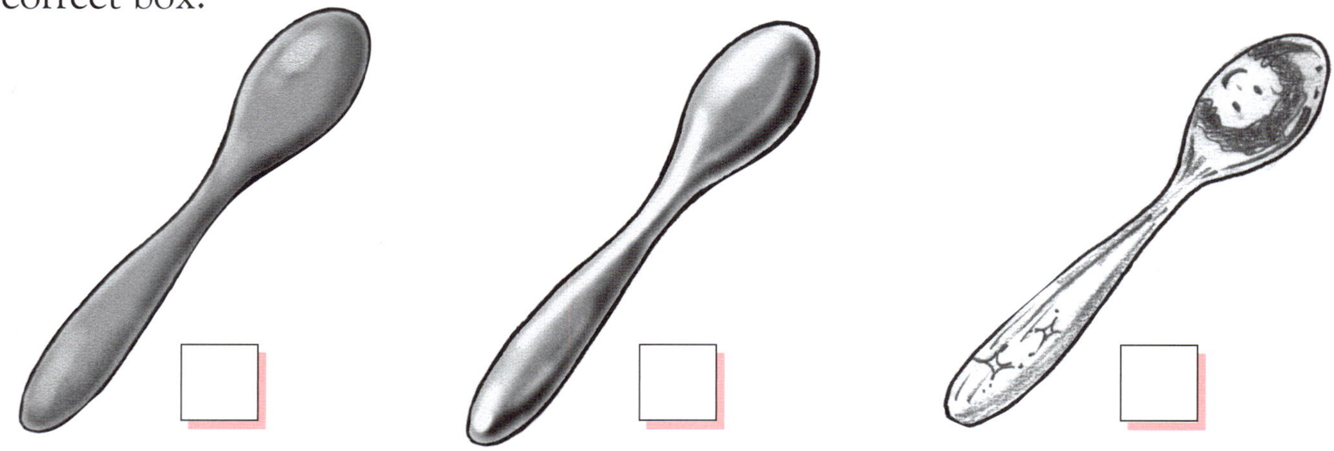

Science investigation

Make your own mirror. Wrap aluminum foil around a small piece of cardboard. Why should you smooth out the foil? Can you see things in the mirror?

2

What makes a thing alive?

Background information

You can tell that something is alive if it can move by itself without being pushed or pulled. Living things eat food. Feeding helps living things to grow and stay healthy. Only living things can *reproduce* (produce offspring). Living things can use their senses of taste, smell, sight, and hearing to react to the world around them.

Science activity

What is each of these living things doing that tells you it is alive? Use one of the words in the box below to complete each sentence.

reproduces	moves	feeds	reacts	grows

I know this horse is alive because it ....

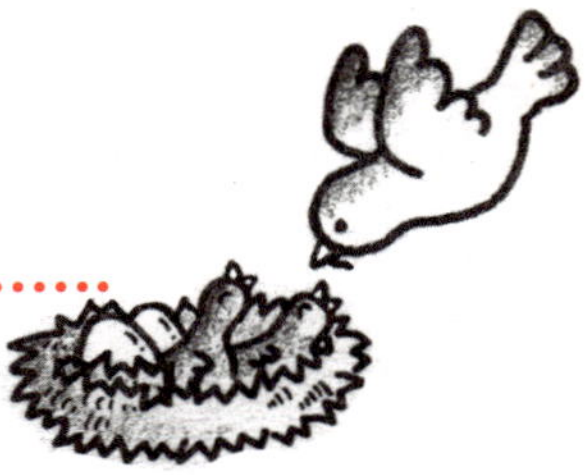

I know this bird is alive because it ....

I know this boy is alive because he ....

I know this caterpillar is alive because it ....

I know this cat is alive because it ....

Science investigation

(!) Feed some lettuce to a land snail or a slug. How does it move?

What kind of an animal is it?

2

Background information

You can recognize different animal groups by the features they have in common. For example, *mammals* have hair on their skin; *birds* have feathers; *reptiles* have scales; *amphibians* have slimy skin; and *fish* have scales and fins.

Science activity

Write which group each animal belongs to and what feature it has that tells you so.

pigeon

A pigeon is a ....

I know because it has ....

lizard

A lizard is a ....

I know because it has ....

cat

A cat is a ....

I know because it has ....

frog

A frog is an ....

I know because it has ....

goldfish

A goldfish is a ....

I know because it has ....

Science investigation

Learn about animal features on the Internet. Which animals are *warm-blooded*, and what does that mean?

What sort of animal is it?

Background information

If you look closely at an animal, you can count how many legs it has. This helps to tell you what sort of animal it is.

Science activity

Count how many legs each of these animals has, then find that number below and follow the wiggly line to find the animal's name.

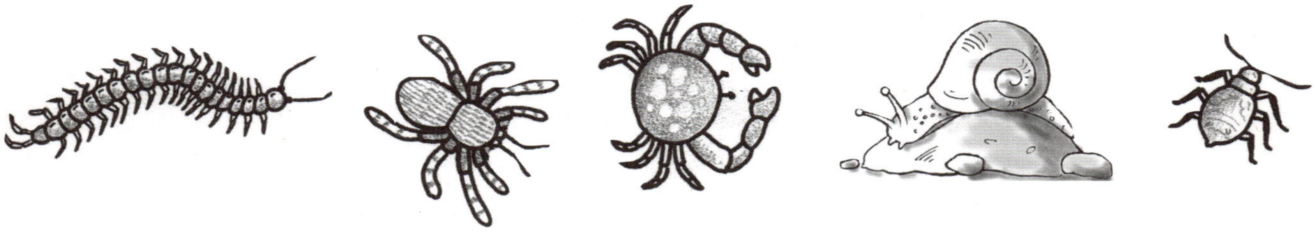

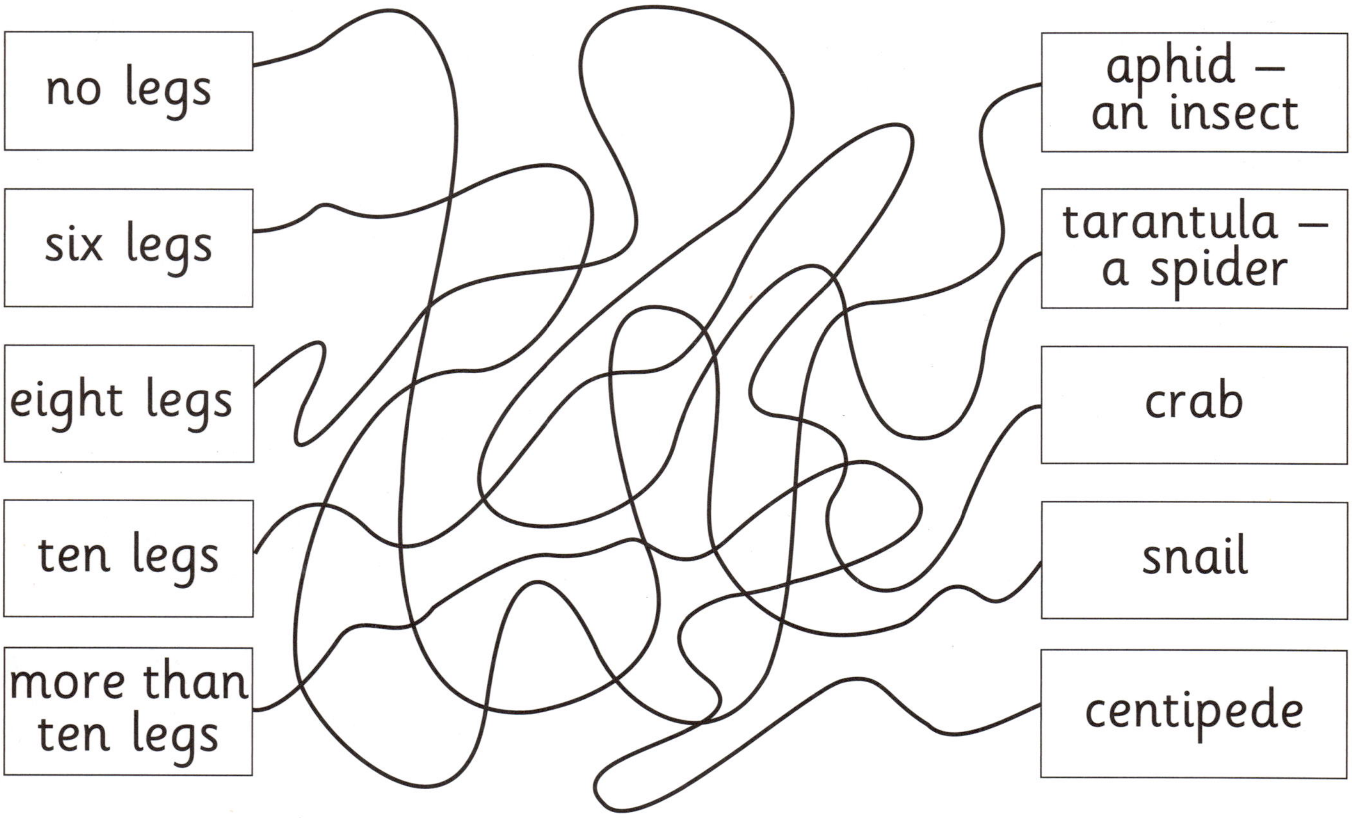

Science investigation

(!) Have an adult help you carefully collect some insects. Place them in a jar. Observe how each one moves. How many legs do insects have? Do they have wings?

How does that live there?

Background information

Animals can live on land, in soil, in water, and in air. Some of these places are wet. Others are dry. Some are in bright light, others are in shade. Different animals are *adapted* to live in different kinds of places. They have certain features that are just right for where they live.

Science activity

1 Colour **orange** one part of a goldfish that helps it live in water.

2 Colour **green** one part of a frog that helps it live in water.

3 Colour **yellow** the part of a duck that helps it live in the air, and colour **blue** a part that helps it live in the water.

Science investigation

(!) If you have the opportunity, go to a garden or park and observe animals in the soil. What types of animals do you think live in the soil? Use a spoon or shovel to move some of the soil. Bring a magnifying glass. Wear gloves when you dig.

☆ 2

Where do animals like to live?

Background information

Animals are found in many different places. Some live in gardens, some live in forests, others live in ponds, or in the ocean.

Science activity

Draw a line joining each animal to the place it lives.

Science investigation

Dig up some soil and place it in a coffee can. Pour the soil over some newspapers and record what you see. Use a magnifying glass to see small critters. Wear plastic gloves.

What is a life cycle?

2

Background information

Adults produce *offspring*. Offspring are young animals, which will one day grow into adults themselves. These adults will then produce offspring of their own. This pattern of events is called a *life cycle*.

Science activity

Here is the life cycle of a chicken. Which picture goes with which stage in the life cycle? Write **A**, **B**, **C**, or **D** in each box.

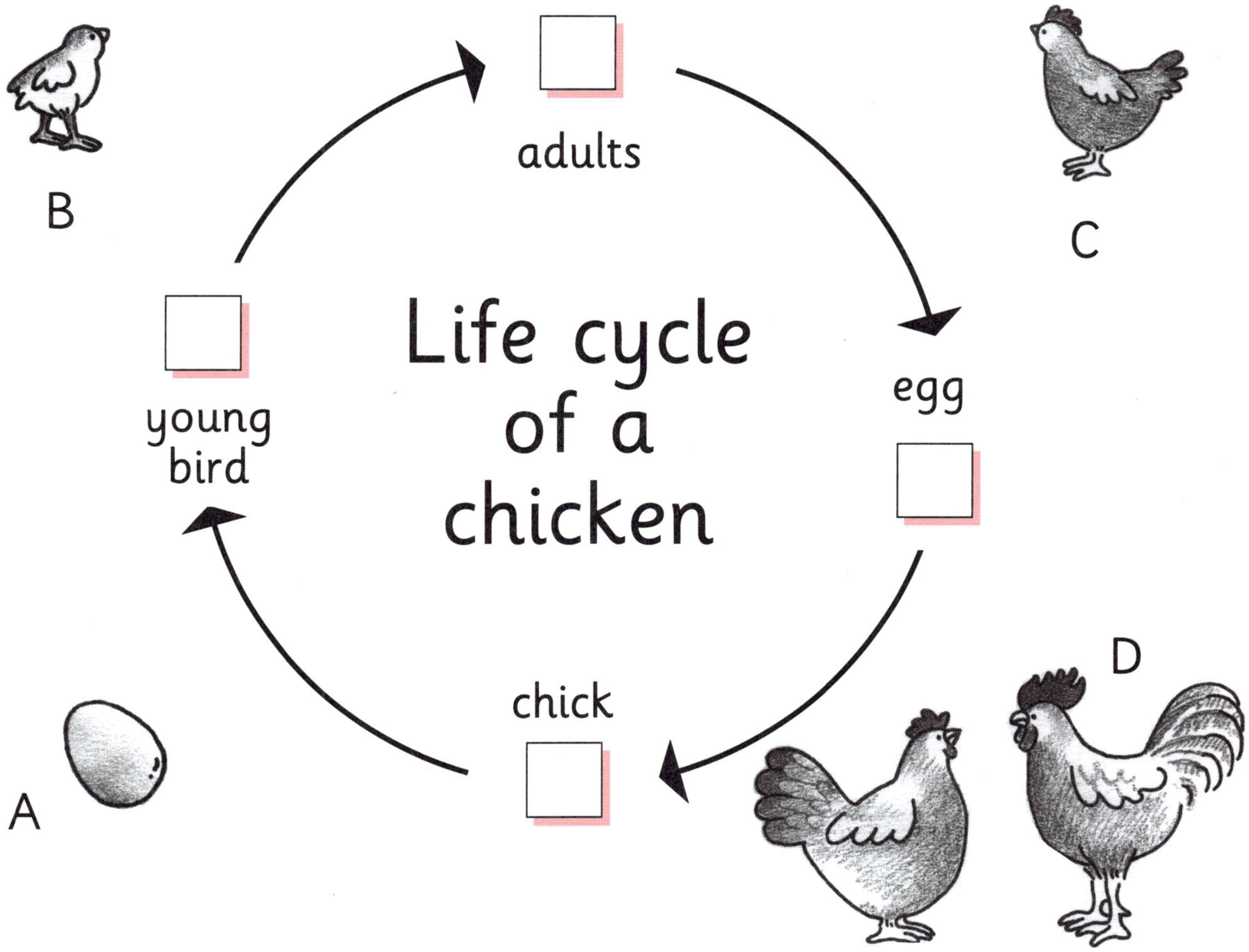

Science investigation

(!) To observe a beetle's cycle, place some mealworms in a jar with a little oatmeal and a cut-up potato. Punch holes in the jar's lid. Observe for two weeks.

2

What is its body like?

Background information

A human's body is covered with smooth skin. Different animals have different types of skin. Some animals have hair or fur; others have feathers. Some have scales and spines. Some have a hard shell.

Science activity

Connect each animal to the type of outer covering it has.

Science investigation

Cover one Styrofoam ball with yarn, stick 20 toothpicks in another, and cover a third with plastic wrap. Which covering best protects these "animals" from enemies? Explain why you think so.

Does it move?

Background information
Living things can move by themselves. Some living things move quickly; others move slowly. Some living things run; others swim, fly, jump, or crawl.

Science activity
Draw a line joining each animal to the word describing how it moves.

slither

crawl

swim

fly

run

jump

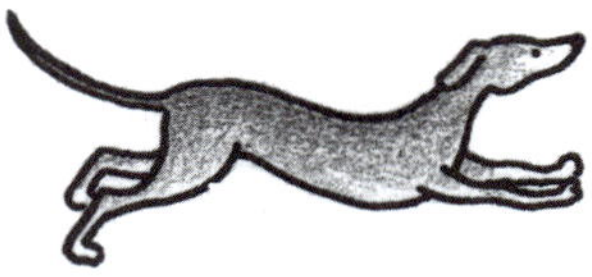

Which of these animals can move by flying?

....

Which of these animals run on four legs?

....

Science investigation

How many different ways can people move? Record how different living things can move.

2 What kind of animal is it?

Background information

There are many different types of animals. Some look alike and some look quite different from one another. One way we can group animals is by the features they have in common. For example, animals that are warm blooded, lay eggs, lack teeth, and have feathers on their body and scales on their legs belong to a group of animals called birds.

Science activity

What features do the animals in each group have in common?
What is the name of each group of animals?

Common features of group A animals:

....

....

....

....

These animals are ....

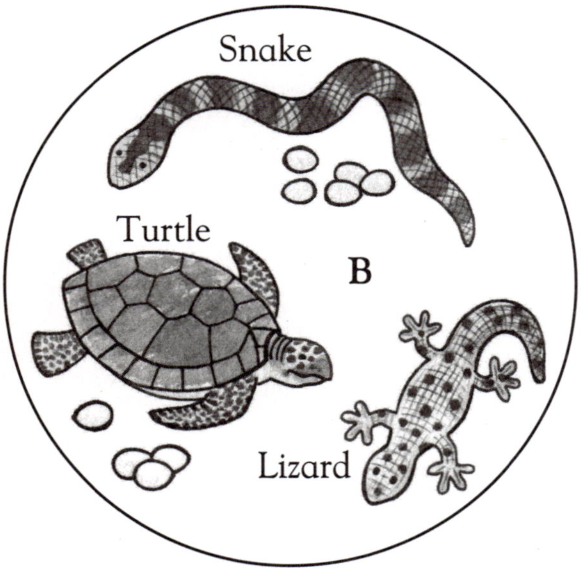

Common features of group B animals:

....

....

....

....

These animals are ....

Science investigation

Place some stuffed animals or animal toys together. Group them by their features. How many groups can you make? What features did you use? Compare your groups to the groups in the activity above.

What makes things go faster?

2

Background information

Pushes and pulls are forces that can make things move faster or slower. Pushes and pulls can also make things stop moving.

Science activity

Answer the questions about making things move faster or slower.

How can Jason make the ball roll slower?

....

How can Amy make the ball move faster?

....

How can Luke make the bike go slower?

....

How can Anna make the ball move faster?

....

Science investigation

Design and conduct an experiment to see how you can make a marble move quickly and slowly through a cardboard tube.

Can it move in water?

Background information

Animals live in many different places. They live on land, under the ground, in the air, in ponds and lakes, and in the ocean. Animals that live in water have special parts, such as fins and flat tails, to help them move. They are *adapted* to where they live.

Science activity

Color in the animals that live in the water most of the time.

Science investigation

Set up a small aquarium for a goldfish. Carefully observe how a fish moves. With use of the Internet, learn about animals who live in water.

Is it metal, wood, or plastic?

Background information

The things around you are made from different materials, such as metal, wood, and plastic. Metals often look shiny. Their colour may have a copper, silver, or golden. Metals can bend without breaking. Wood does not feel cold to the touch and breaks when bent. Plastics can be shiny and smooth. Some plastics will break when bent and others will not. When you tap wood, metal, or plastic, they all make different types of sounds – "ching," "clunk," or "thud."

Science activity

Help Demetrius decide if these objects are made of metal, wood, or plastic. First write the words **metal**, **wood**, and **plastic** on the dotted lines. Then draw a line joining each object to the correct word.

....

Science investigation

Feel and look at your toys. Which toys are made of plastic? Wood? Metal? Are any made of other material? Make a table to organize your findings.

Why do we use that material?

Background information

When a house is built, materials such as wood, metal, plastic, and clay are used. Each material is chosen because it does a particular job well. For example, clay is used to make bricks because baked clay is strong and does not let water through quickly.

Science activity

Draw a line joining each sentence on the left to the words on the right that describe that material's use.

Wood planks make good floors	because it lets light through.
Glass is used to glaze windows	because it does not rot.
Metal girders are used in buildings	because they're flat and smooth.
Clay is used to make roof tiles	because they're very strong.
Plastic is used for window frames	because it's waterproof.

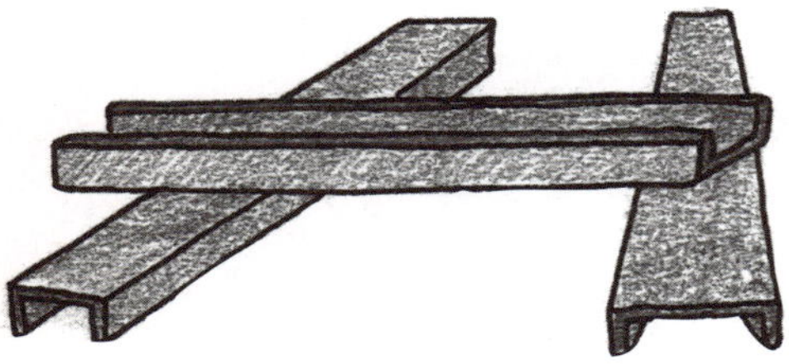

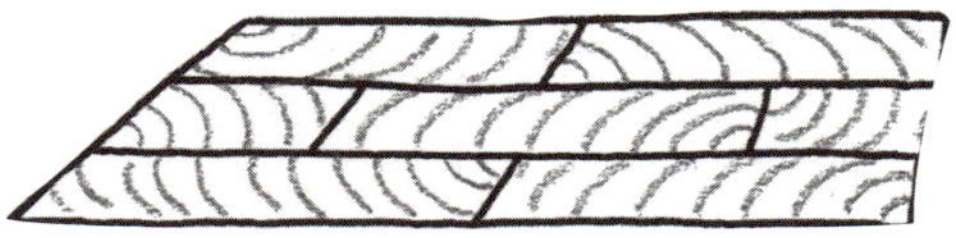

Science investigation

Design and conduct an experiment to see which type of paper is the strongest of these: newspaper, tissue paper, paper towels, or writing paper.

Can you see through it?

2

Background information

You can see through some materials, but not others. If you shine a flashlight on a material that is not see-through, light cannot pass through it. Some materials are not see-through, but if light is shined on one of side of them, a glow can be seen on the other side.

Science activity

Place a check mark (✔) in the correct box to show if you think each material is see-through, not see-through, or is not see-through but you can see a flashlight glow through it.

Material	See-through	Not see-through	See flashlight glow
kitchen foil			
plastic cling film			
tissues			
wooden toy			
glass window			
cloth handkerchief			
glass of water			

Science investigation

Obtain different types of paper. Predict and test which ones are see-through and which ones are not see-through. Were any materials partly see-through?

2

Which is the best material to use?

Background information

When you make something, it is important to use materials that are right for the job. You would not make a bicycle out of tissue paper or a book out of metal. The owners of factories that make new things ask scientists to carry out tests to find the best materials to use.

Science activity

A factory owner wanted to know which fabric he should use to make swimsuits that dry quickly. He asked a scientist to do a test. She made four swimsuits of the same size from different materials, then rinsed them in water and left them to dry. Here are her results.

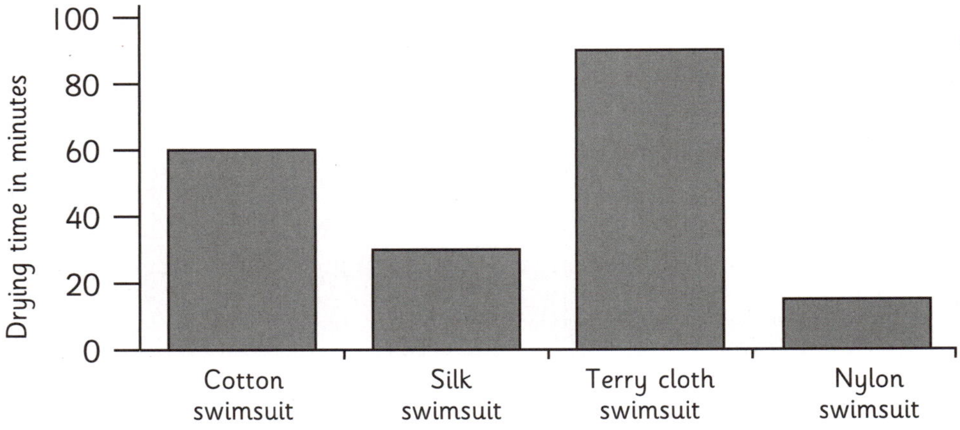

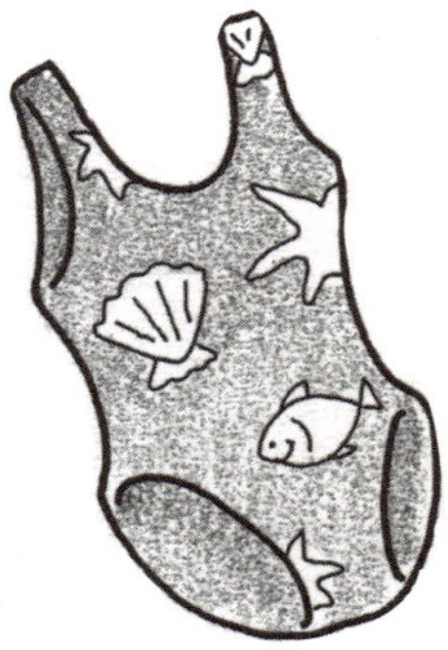

1 Which material should the factory owner choose? ....

2 Why is that the best choice? ....

3 Why did the scientist make all the swimsuits the same size?

....

Science investigation

Design and conduct an experiment to see which material—cotton, paper, aluminum foil, or vinyl—would be best for making an easy-to-clean painting apron. What parts of your experiment will have to be kept the same?

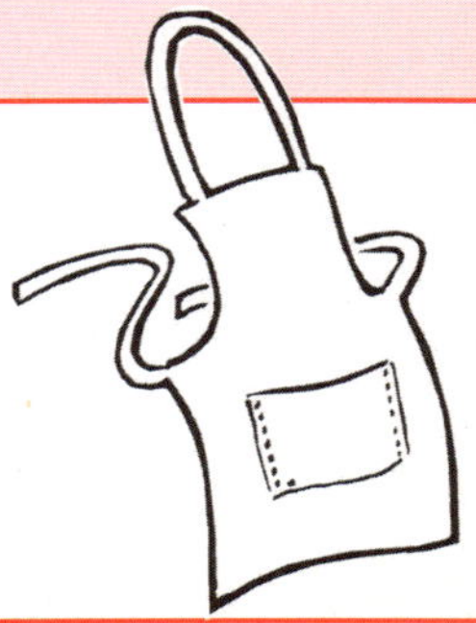

Will it keep you dry?

Background information

Many different materials are used to build houses. Slate is a hard rock that splits easily into thin sheets. Bricks and tiles are made from clay that is baked in a kiln. Glass, made from sand, is used for windowpanes. Window frames and doors are made of wood or plastic. Building materials need to be *waterproof* to stop water coming through the roof, walls, windows, and floors.

Science activity

Jamal and Chessie stood pieces of different materials in bowls of water to find out which ones were waterproof. After a few days, they looked to see how far the water had risen up each sample. Here are the results.

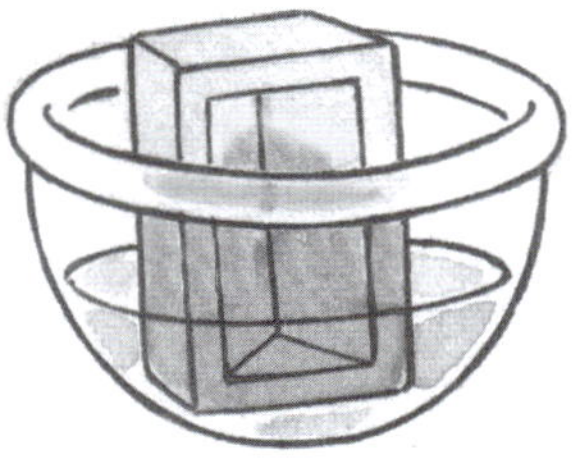
Brick

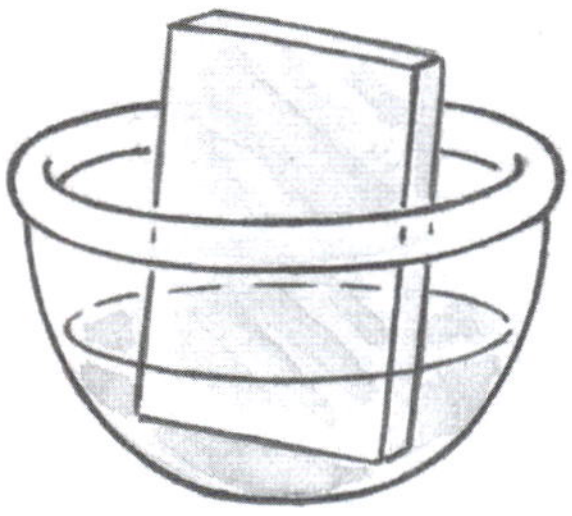
Glass

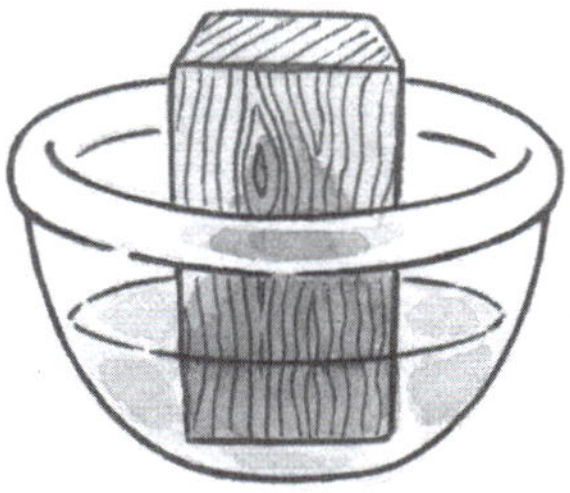
Wood

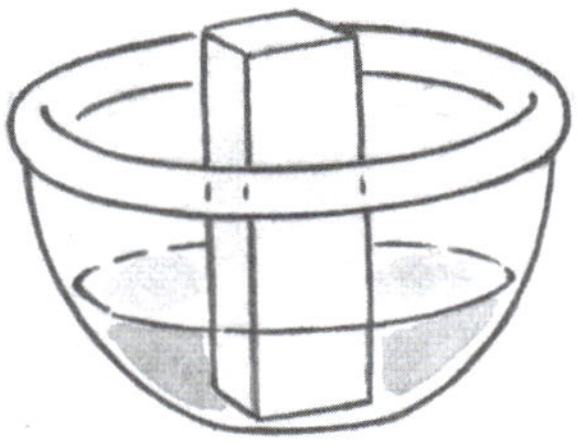
Plastic

Slate

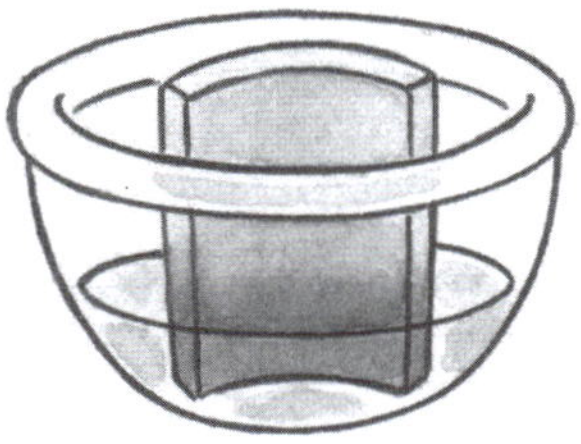
Tile

Which materials are the most waterproof? Explain. ....

....

Which materials are the least waterproof? Explain. ....

....

Science investigation

Design and conduct an experiment to decide what type of fabric should be used to make a raincoat, or to see which of your family's raincoats keeps the rain off the best. Ask an adult to help you obtain samples of fabrics, or to use the family raincoats.

Does it float?

2

Background information

When you place things in water, some of them *float* and some of them *sink*. Things that float stay on top of the water. Things that sink go to the bottom of the water.

Science activity

Here are some pieces of fruit that have been placed in a bowl of water. Colour the ones that float blue and those that sink, red.

Science investigation

Gather some small objects. Predict whether they will float or sink, and then test your prediction by placing each one in a bowl of water.

Does it change when it is hot?

2

Background information

Some things respond to heat by getting runny. They are *melting,* just like your ice cream cone on a sunny day. They are changing from a solid to a liquid.

Science activity

Write an **M** by the things that melt when they are put into warm places.

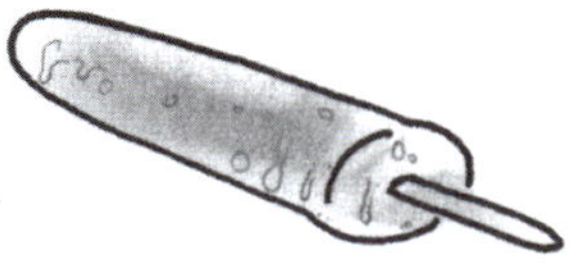

☐ popsicle

☐ metal spoon

☐ Jell-O

☐ teapot

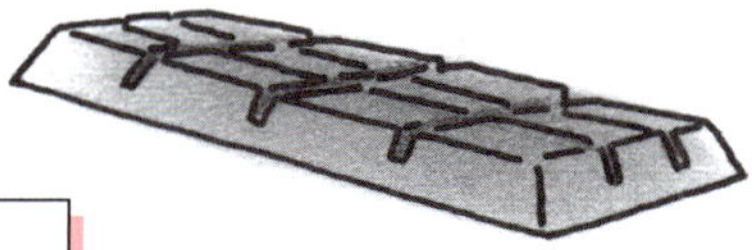

☐ chocolate bar

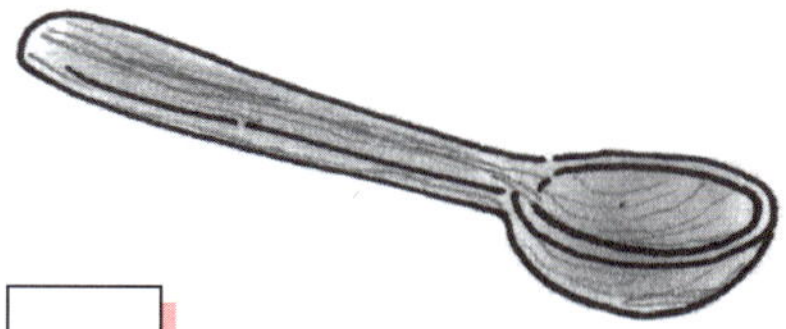

☐ wooden spoon

☐ butter

☐ candle

Science investigation

What happens to an ice cube placed in an empty cup in your room and left there for a while?

☆2 Does it change when it is cold?

Background information

Some things change when they are cooled. For example, some things become solid in cold places. When a material *freezes*, it turns from a liquid to a solid.

Science activity

Place a check mark (✔) in the box next to the correct answer to each question. The first one is done for you.

Which one is easier to mold into things?

☐ Clay or plasticene kept in a cool place

☑ Clay or plasticene kept in a warm place

Which is easier to spread on bread?

☐ Butter from the fridge

☐ Butter left out at room temperature

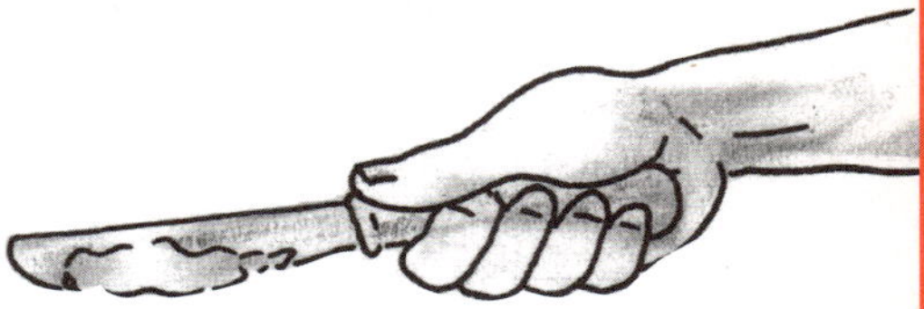

Which one feels harder?

☐ Water from the faucet

☐ Water left in the freezer overnight

Which one is easier to break?

☐ Chocolate just removed from the fridge

☐ Chocolate held in your hands for a few minutes

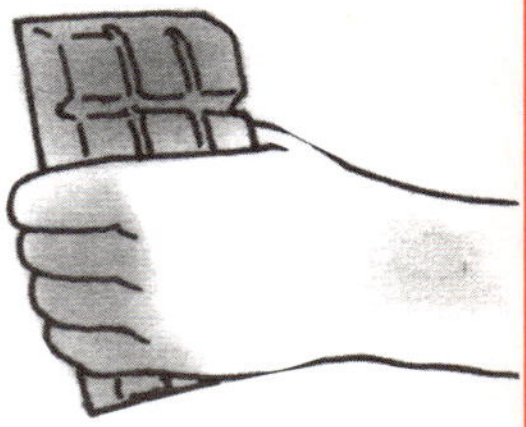

Which one is more runny?

☐ Ice cream from the freezer

☐ Ice cream you have been eating for a few minutes

Science investigation

Place some clay or plasticene in the freezer and some in the fridge. Leave some at room temperature. Compare their differences.

What cools the quickest?

2

Background information

When things are heated, they become hot. When heat is taken away, they cool down. Some things cool quickly, others cool more slowly.

Science activity

Jeffrey baked some cakes in a very hot oven at 180°C. He took them out of the oven and left them to cool. After ten minutes, he stuck a thermometer inside each cake. Place a check mark (✔) in the box by the cake that cooled the quickest.

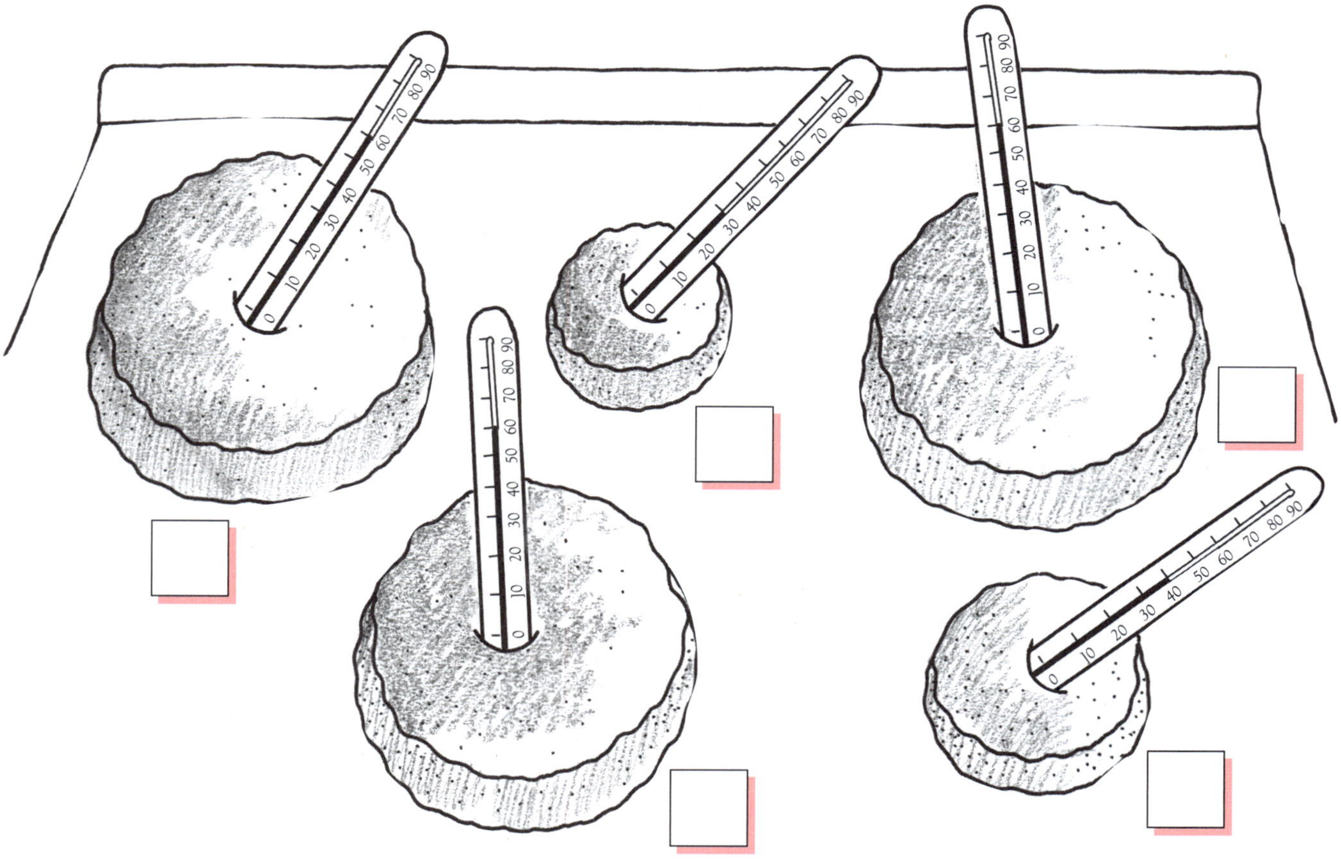

Science investigation

(!) Record the temperature of just-prepared Jell-O every 30 minutes, until it becomes solid. How does the temperature change?

Does it change forever?

Background information

When you leave water in the freezer, it changes into ice: it changes from a liquid to a solid. When you take the ice out of the freezer, it changes back into water. When you cook an egg, it changes from being runny to being a solid. You can unfreeze the ice, but you cannot "uncook" the egg. Some changes can go back and forth, others cannot.

Science activity

Look at this kitchen. Draw a circle around each food item that changes when you heat it and then changes back again when it cools down. Place an (✘) over each food item that changes when you heat it, but does not change back when it cools down.

Science investigation

(!) Make some Jell-O with the help of an adult. Next, make some whipped cream. Can either of these foods change back into a liquid again?

Will it ever change back?

Background information

When ice cream melts, you can make it hard again by cooling it in a freezer. You can make frozen ice cream soft by heating it up. These changes can be reversed (changed back). When a match burns, it changes into ash and smoke. You cannot change the ash and smoke back into a match. This change cannot be reversed.

Science activity

For each of the changes described below, draw a circle around the **H** if the change can be reversed by heating, around the **C** if the change can be reversed by cooling, and around the **N** if it can never be reversed.

Charcoal is burned on a barbecue. H, C or N?

Jell-O hardens in the refrigerator. H, C, or N?

Flour, eggs, sugar, and butter are made into a cake. H, C, or N?

Butter becomes soft in the dish. H, C, or N?

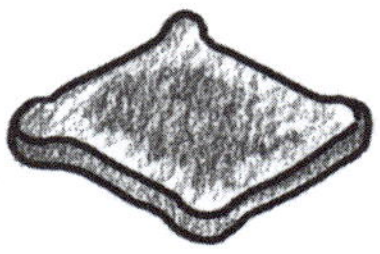

Bread is made into toast. H, C, or N?

Water turns to ice in the freezer. H, C, or N?

Chocolate melts and becomes runny. H, C, or N?

Science investigation

What happens to candies when placed in water? Place one candy in each of three different see-through cups and cover each with 100 ml of water. Is the reaction reversible?

2

Does it make a circuit?

Background information

Bulbs, buzzers, and motors all have two ends where wires can be attached. To make them work, both ends must be connected to a battery. Batteries also have two ends, one is marked with a positive sign (+) and the other, with a negative sign (–). Always have an adult help you when you work with batteries. Here is a picture of a circuit. All the parts are joined, and the bulb is lit up.

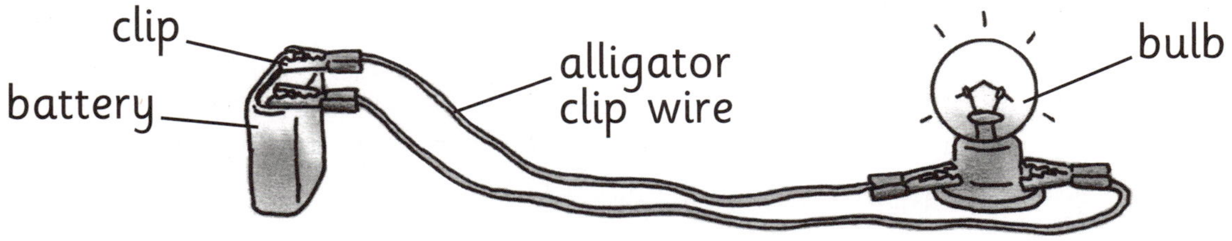

Science activity

There is a part missing from both of these circuits, which means they do not work. Draw in the part needed to make each circuit work.

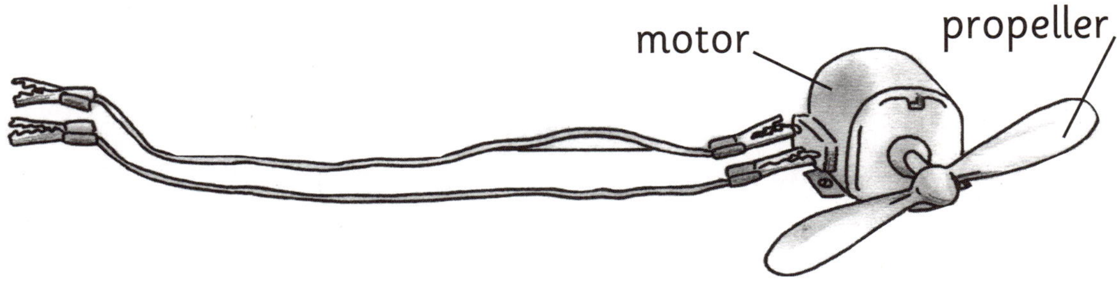

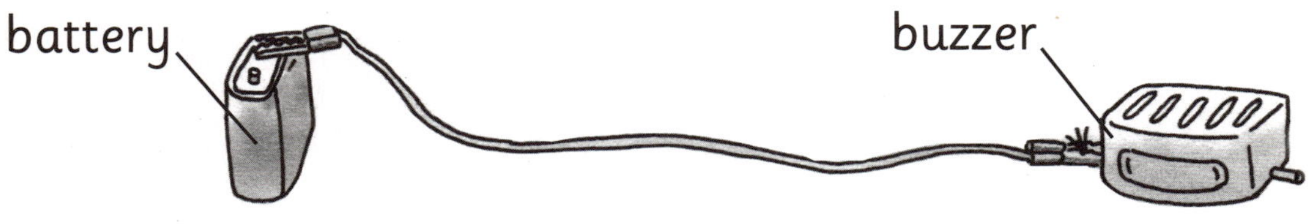

Science investigation

(!) Ask a grown-up for a 1.5 volt battery, two 1.5 volt bulbs, and three alligator wires. Connect all the parts together so that both bulbs light up.

Which one moves the fastest?

Background information

A push is a *force*. A pull is also a force. Forces can make things move. They can also slow things down. Some forces can make things move fast. They can make some things move faster than others.

Science activity

Samantha is playing with a ball. Colour in the pictures where she is making the ball move fast.

throwing

kicking

holding

bouncing

sitting

Which activity makes the ball go the fastest? ....

Science investigation

Drop marbles from different heights onto flattened clay or plasticene. What happens to the clay?

2

Does it roll, slide, or fall?

Background information
Living things can move by themselves. Things that are not alive move in different ways. Some things fall; some things roll; some things fly; some things slide; some things bounce; and some things pour.

Science activity
Draw a line joining each picture to the word that describes how it is moving.

bounce

roll

slide

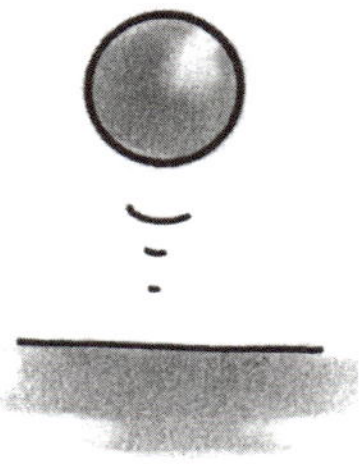

fly

fall

pour

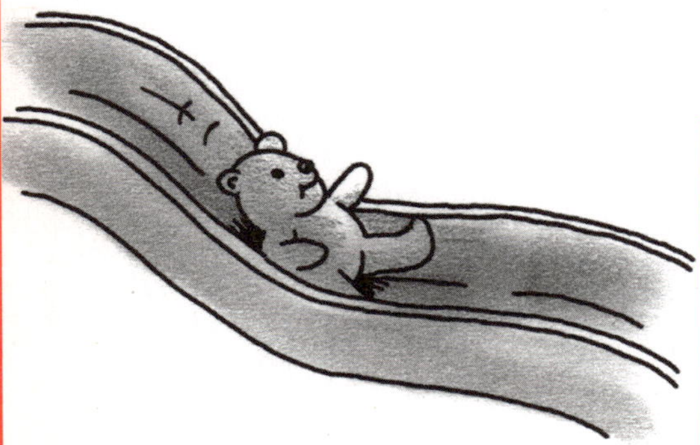

Science investigation

Observe and record how things move at a playground. Try moving in different ways. Can a ball move in some of the ways you do?

Is it a push or a pull?

2

Background information

Things move when you push them and pull them. A push or a pull is a *force* that causes things to go faster or slower, or to stop. When you are very forceful (you give a hard push), you can make a toy car go fast. When you are not so forceful (soft push), the car will go slowly.

Science activity

Do these things need a push or a pull to make them move? Write push or pull under each picture.

Science investigation

(!) Predict and test what you think will happen if you give a toy car a hard push and then a soft push. Try this with different-sized cars.

How do things start and stop?

Background information

Pushes and pulls are *forces.* When you push or pull something, you can make it start or stop moving.

Science activity

Look at each picture. Is the child in each picture using a pushing force or a pulling force? Write **push** or **pull** on the first line. Does the force cause something to start or stop moving? Write **start** or **stop** on the second line.

....

....

....

....

....

....

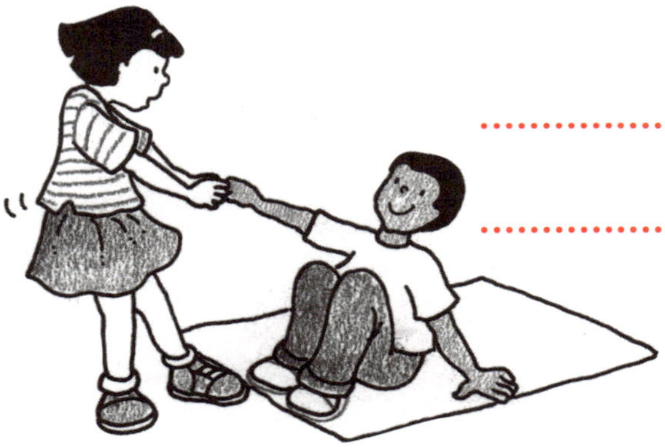

....

....

....

....

Science investigation

Play tug-of-war with a friend. Are you pushing or pulling? Kick a soccer ball. What type of force will stop the ball?

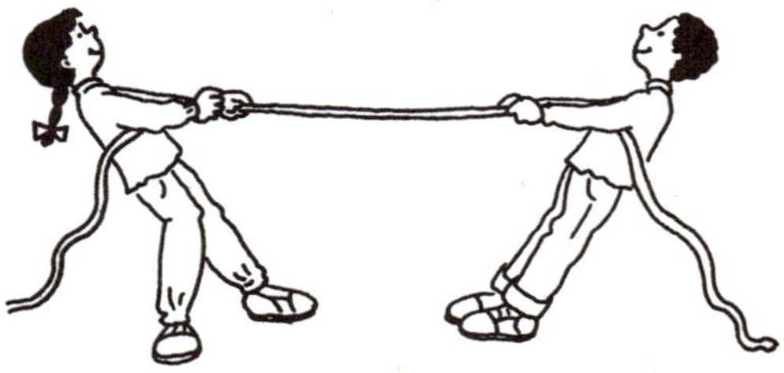

Why do things change direction?

Background information

Pushes and pulls are forces. Forces can make moving things change direction. If you blow at a table tennis ball that is rolling towards you, the ball will change direction. When you blow, your breath provides the forces to push the ball.

Science activity

Write **yes** or **no** beside each picture below to say whether or not the player is using a force that will make the ball change direction.

....

....

....

....

....

Science investigation

(!) Design and conduct an experiment to see if it is easier to push a water-filled balloon or air-filled balloon into a basin of water.

2

What makes it work?

Background information

Many things need *electricity* to work. *Batteries* are one source of electricity. Electricity can also be obtained by plugging things into a socket in the wall. This electricity comes from wires that go into your home. Never place anything but an electrical plug into a socket or you can receive an electric shock that can kill or badly hurt you!

Science activity

Which of these things work when they are plugged into a wall socket? Which ones work with batteries? Draw a line joining each one to the correct word. The first one is done for you.

socket | batteries

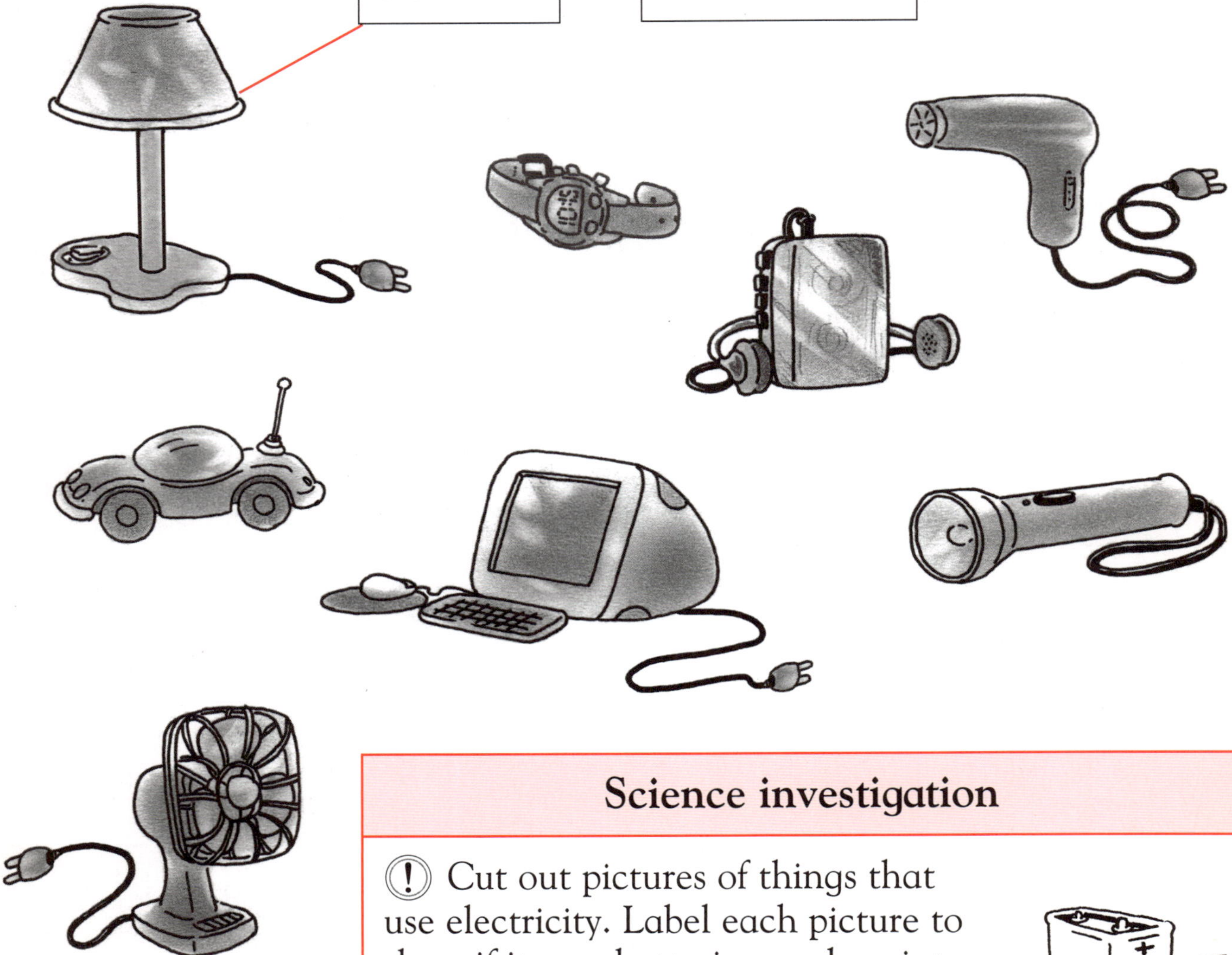

Science investigation

(!) Cut out pictures of things that use electricity. Label each picture to show if it uses batteries or plugs into a socket.

Can electricity be dangerous?

2

Background information

To use a hair dryer, you must first plug it into a wall socket. Electricity from the socket makes the dryer work. You must be very careful when plugging things into a socket. Never touch the metal pins at the end of a plug, and never touch anything electrical with wet hands, because you can get an electric shock. Electric shocks can hurt or even kill you. You must also be careful with electricity as it can cause fires.

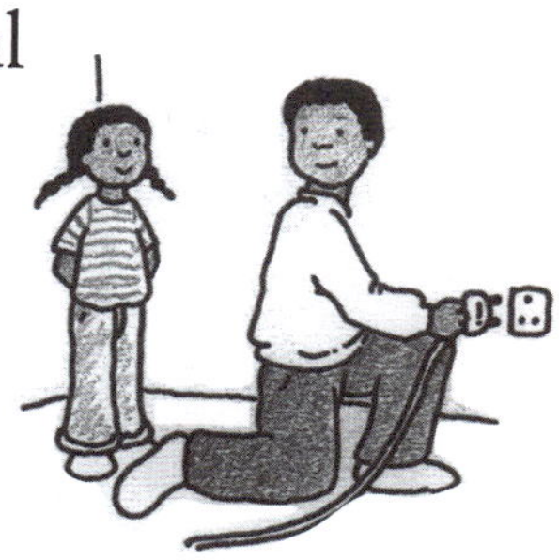

Science activity

Write **yes** or **no** to answer each of these questions.

1 Can electricity give you a shock? ....

2 Can electricity kill you? ....

3 Can electricity cause a fire? ....

4 Should you always use batteries for your experiments at home? ....

5 Should you ever play with electric plugs or wall sockets? ....

6 Should you put wires into electrical wall sockets? ....

7 Should you use plugs and wall sockets for experiments at home? ....

8 Should you always ask an adult before plugging something into a wall socket? ....

Science investigation

(!) How many devices are plugged into each electrical outlet in your home? Is this safe?

SCIENCE WORD POWER

Example

Fill in the shapes with pictures or words related to the science word.

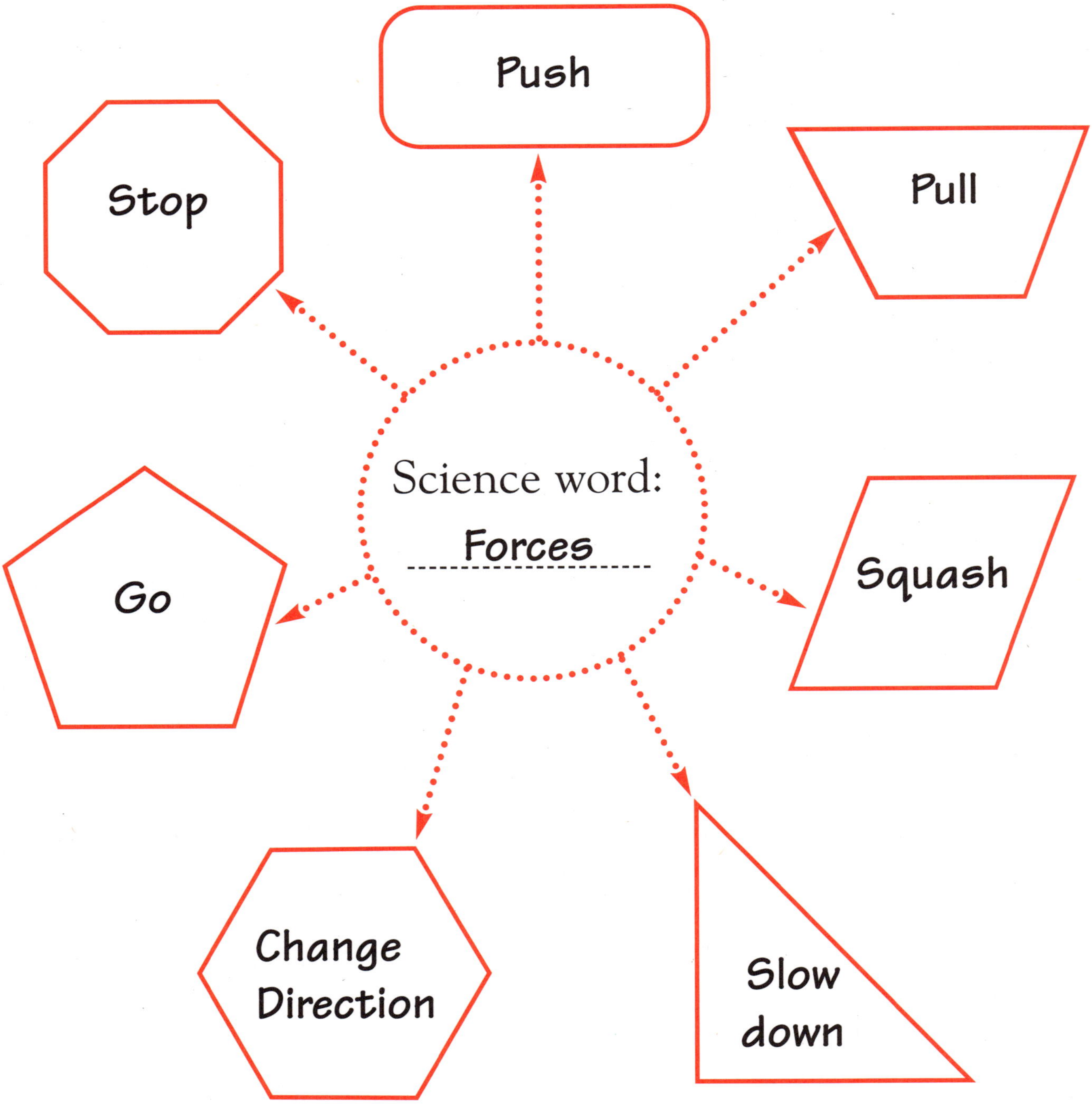

SCIENCE WORD POWER

Fill in the shapes with pictures or words related to the science word.

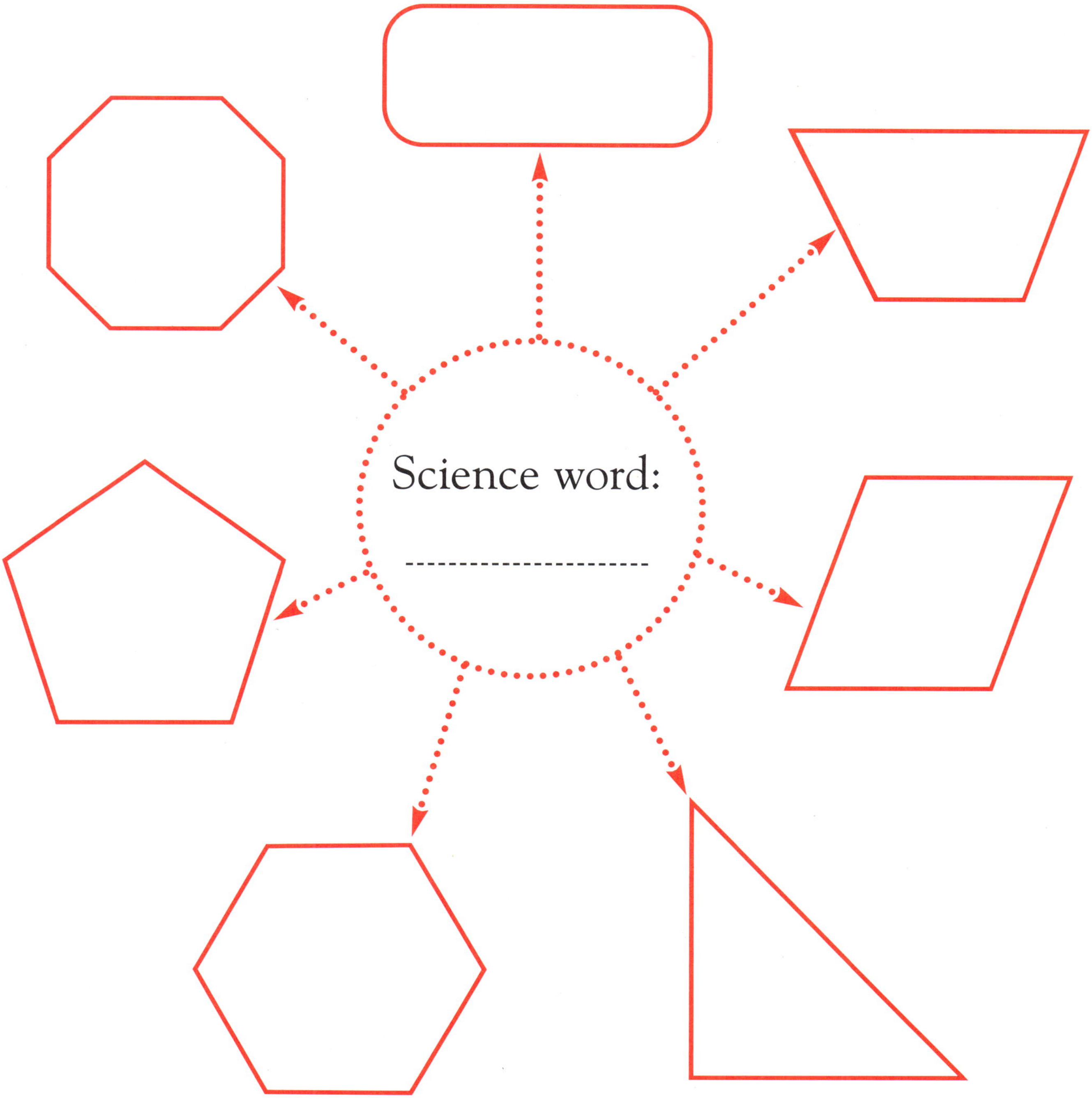

Inquiry template

The adult in charge should use this template to guide the child through the activities and explorations.

Name .... Date ....

Period of exploration: Give the young learner some experience in manipulating objects. For example, a child manipulating a mirror will observe some of the properties of light without realizing it.

Form a question: Manipulate a mirror or other objects as a means of generating questions. Encourage the learner to say, " I wonder..."

Make a plan: The learner develops a plan for his or her investigation. What materials will be needed? The adult should provide some support in helping to direct the child's plan by carefully observing the learner and providing suggestions.

Investigate: The learner carries out the designed plan.

Record and report: Depending on the child's level of writing and reading, he or she should give a report verbally and/or written out. Encourage pictures (diagrams).

Reflect, revisit, and plan again: Was the learner surprised by the results? Could he or she have improved the experiment? What other questions does the learner have?

Questions for adults to consider:

Before activity

1. How does this activity relate to the provincial curriculum guidelines? (If you are not familiar with the guidelines, check the Ministry of Education's Internet site.)

2. What skills are being developed?

After Activity

1. What went well?

2. What needs to be modified?

Inquiry template

The adult in charge should use this template to guide the child through the activities and explorations.

Name .... Date ....

Period of exploration:

Form a question:

Make a plan:

Investigate:

Record and report:

Reflect, revisit, and plan again:

Questions for adults to consider:

Before activity

1. How does this activity relate to the provincial curriculum guidelines? (If you are not familiar with the guidelines, check the Ministry of Education's Internet site.)
2. What skills are being developed?

After Activity

1. What went well?
2. What needs to be modified?

Answer Section with Notes for Adults

Grades K-2

This section provides answers and explanatory notes for all of the science activities and investigations. Ensure that all safety precautions are carefully followed. Be aware of toxic and flammable chemicals. Proceed carefully when using an open flame or heating device.

When appropriate, use the inquiry template to guide the child through the investigations in a manner that parallels how science is done in the real world. The graphic organizer should be used to help the child to better understand scientific concepts while building vocabulary.

8

Where is your nose? Where are your toes?

Background information
Your body is made up of lots of parts. You have a head, a body (or trunk), two arms, and two legs. Each of these parts is made up of other smaller parts, such as your nose and toes.

Science activity
Use these words to name the different parts of the body.
Write the words on the lines.

head arm leg trunk knee toe elbow hand nose

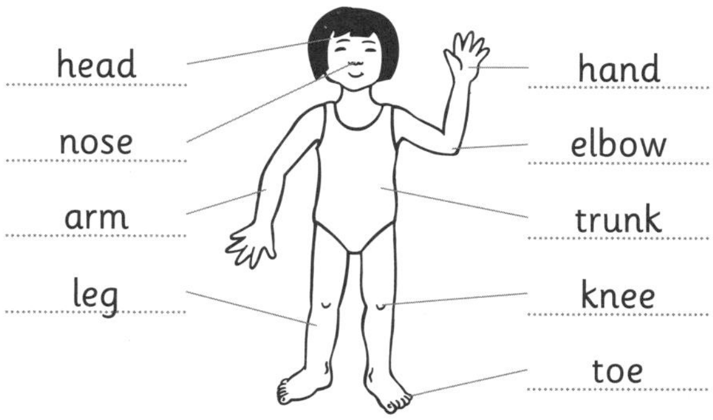

Science investigation

Draw a face with hair, eyes, nose, ears, cheeks, mouth, and a chin.

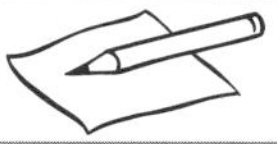

Can your child name the main parts of the body? You might need to write the words and let your child write over them. If your child looks into a mirror before the drawing activity, it will help with identifying different parts of the face.

9

Can you find the eyes?

Background information
Many animals have eyes. They use them to see. Some eyes are in funny places. Some animals have no eyes at all!

Science activity
Do all these animals have eyes? Find their eyes and circle them.

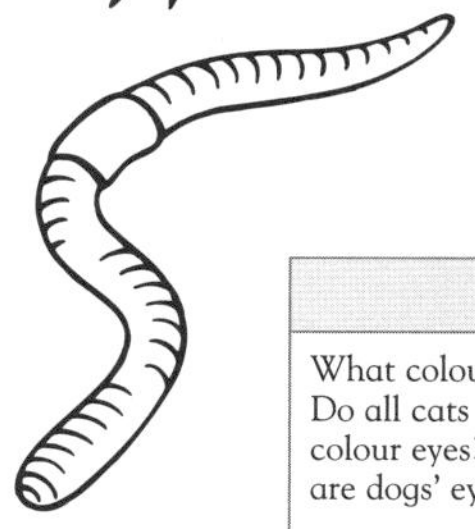

Science investigation

What colour are cats' eyes? Do all cats have the same colour eyes? What colour are dogs' eyes?

Many animals, such as zoo and farm animals, have eyes similar to ours. Encourage your child to look for eyes and describe them when he or she is around animals. If appropriate, tell your child that worms do not have eyes but are sensitive to light.

10

What can you hear?

Background information
You use your ears to listen. Lots of different things make sounds. Sometimes you can hear very quiet sounds. Sometimes you can hear very noisy sounds.

Science activity
Find the things in this picture that make a sound.
Draw a line from each one to the girl's ear.

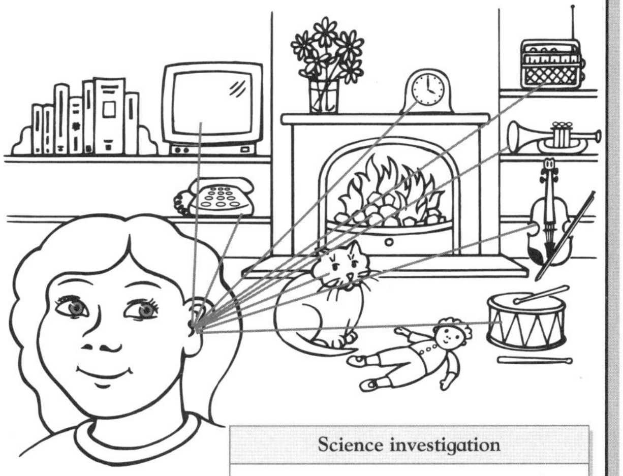

Science investigation

(!) Make a string telephone.
Listen for sounds through your telephone.

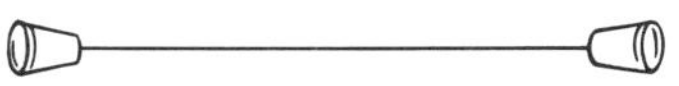

Your child will learn that the ear hears different types of sound. You will need to help your child make the string-cup telephone, especially piercing the holes. For the telephone to work, the string must be taut.

11

How does sound vary?

Background information
You use your ears to hear sounds. Some sounds are loud and easy to hear. Other sounds are quiet and hard to hear. Some sounds are so loud they hurt your ears. People can wear ear protectors to protect their hearing in places where sounds are very loud.

Science activity
If you stood next to each of these things, which one would sound the loudest? Place a check mark (✔) on the box beside it. Which one would sound the quietest? Put an (✘) in the box beside it. Circle the one that is so loud you would need to wear ear protectors to stand near it.

Science investigation

Place some popcorn on a wooden cutting board. What happens when you tap harder and harder with a wooden spoon?

The child will learn that the loudness of sound varies. As the child taps harder, the sound becomes louder and the popcorn will jump higher and higher. Ask the child what he or she feels against his or her hand. The child should feel the vibrations of the board.

12

Does it smell nice?

Background information
Some smells are nice, some are nasty. Everybody has favourite smells. Which smells do you like?

Science activity
Which of these smells do you think are nice, and which ones do you think are nasty? Draw a ☺ if it is nice and ☹ if it is not.

Science investigation

(!) What does it look like inside your nose? Use a small flashlight and mirror to find out – but never put anything up your nose!

Does your child have favourite smells among those in the science activity? Using a mirror or flashlight will enable closer observation of the nose. You can explain that the nose is also used for breathing air in and out.

13

What tastes best?

Background information
You use your tongue to taste things. Some things taste sweet, some taste salty. Some things taste sour and others taste bitter.

Science activity
How do these things taste? Draw a line from each picture to the word that matches its taste.

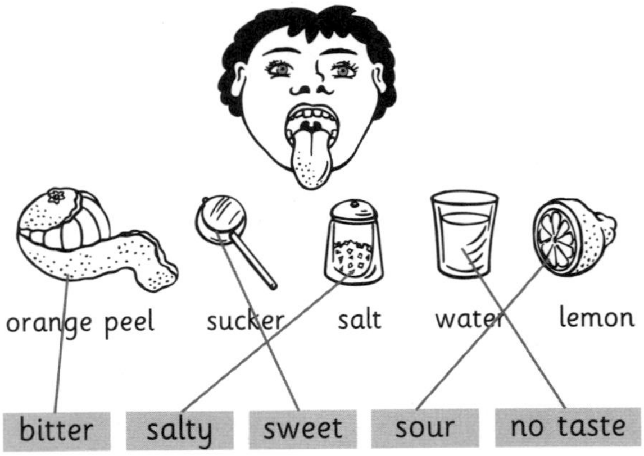

Science investigation

Can you tell the difference between salty, sour, and sweet things if you close your eyes and hold your nose when you taste them? With an adult, investigate with different foods.

Your child will learn that the tongue is used for tasting. The tastes *sour* and *bitter* are hard to distinguish, and your child may confuse the two. You might like to discuss how the senses of smell and taste are linked.

14

What does it feel like?

Background information
You touch things with your fingers to find out what they feel like. You can also feel things with other parts of your body, such as your elbows or your toes.

Science activity
What would you feel if you touched each of these things?

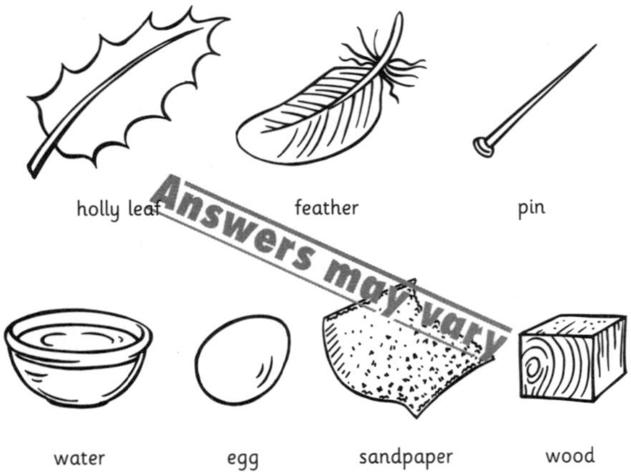

Science investigation

(!) Close your eyes and see if you can tell what something is just by the way it feels.

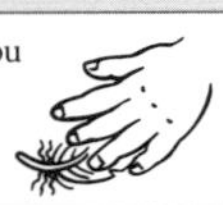

This page introduces the sense of touch. The activity might produce a good range of describing words, such as *prickly* and *slimy*. To extend the activity, a fun game is to see if your child can feel and name things with their eyes closed using only their toes!

15

Is it light or heavy?

Background information
You can use your hands to feel if something is light or if it is heavy. Heavy things are more difficult to carry. Some things are so heavy that you need a crane to lift them.

Science activity
Draw a ring around each light thing.

Which thing is the lightest? Which is the heaviest?

Science investigation

Find something that is as heavy as a bag of sugar.

Introducing the opposites of light and heavy may help your child in this activity. Begin to make comparisons, such as *lighter than* or *heavier than* when your child is finding something that is as heavy as a bag of sugar.

16

Do all living things grow?

Background information
Are you growing bigger? All living things grow. When you eat, your body uses some of the food to help you grow.

Science activity
Place a check mark (✔) in the box beside each picture that shows a living thing growing bigger.

Science investigation

Have an adult measure your height at least once a week. Are you growing? Explain. Keep track of your height. Record the date each time it is measured.

The child should understand that all living things grow. Placing the objects in chronological order will help reinforce this concept. Ask the child to explain how the "growing" balloon differs from the growing bird.

17

Do you look like your parents?

Background information
All animals can make more of themselves. They do this by *reproducing* themselves. Male and female animals are needed to produce the young or *offspring*. Young animals eat and grow into adult animals.

Science activity
Draw lines to connect the male, female, and young in each family.

Science investigation

Some adults look very different from when they were young. Learn about growing frogs using resource books or the Internet.

The child learns that humans and other animals produce offspring that grow into adults. Help the child with new vocabulary. Some offspring, like tadpoles, do not resemble their parents when young. Other resources, such as books and the Internet, should help the child understand this.

18

Do all living things reproduce?

Background information
Have you ever seen a puppy? Puppies are the babies of dogs. Dogs and all living things make more of themselves by *reproducing*.

Science activity
Draw a line joining each parent to its baby. The first one is done for you.

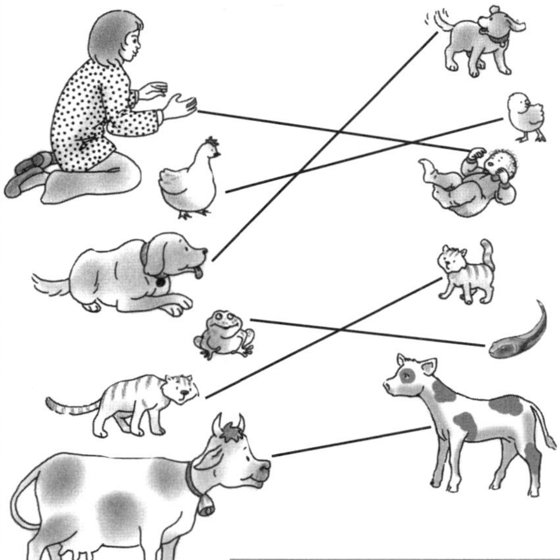

Science investigation

How are baby and adult animals alike and different? Show this in a scrapbook.

Help the child make a scrapbook of babies and their parents. The child should see that babies look different from their parents, but can usually be matched up. Point out that some baby animals, such as frogs, look very different from the adult animal.

19

What does it taste like?

Background information
Many living things taste their food with their tongues. Some animals twist their tongues to smell food

Science activity
Draw an (✘) on the tongues of these living things.
What does each one like to eat?

Science investigation

(!) Close your eyes, hold your nose, and taste various foods. Can you tell them apart? Try again without holding your nose.

The child will learn about the sense of taste. Be aware of allergies; for safety do not use peanuts. Make liquid solutions of sugar and salt. Use lemon juice or vinegar for a sour flavour. Dip a clean Q-tip into each liquid and then place it on the child's tongue.

20

What body parts does a plant have?

Background information
A plant has a body, which is called a stem. Instead of arms and legs, it has leaves and roots. Many plants have flowers as well.

Science activity
Be a plant detective and name the parts of the plant from the clues. Draw a line from each clue to the right word.

Clues	Words
This part is often very colourful.	stem
This part is green and flat.	root
This part is below the ground.	leaf
This part is green, thin and grows upwards.	flower

Science investigation

With an adult, visit a garden, park, or shop.
How many different types of flower can you see?

Reading and discussing the clues in this activity will help your child name the main parts of a plant. A visit to a garden, park, or flower shop may increase your child's general knowledge of plant names.

21

What makes it grow?

Background information
Beans and peas are seeds. To make a seed grow, you must give it water and soil, and you must keep it warm. When it starts to grow, you must keep it in the light.

Science activity
This bean seed was planted a few weeks ago. Can you put the pictures in the correct order to show how the bean grew? Write the letters in the correct order on the line.

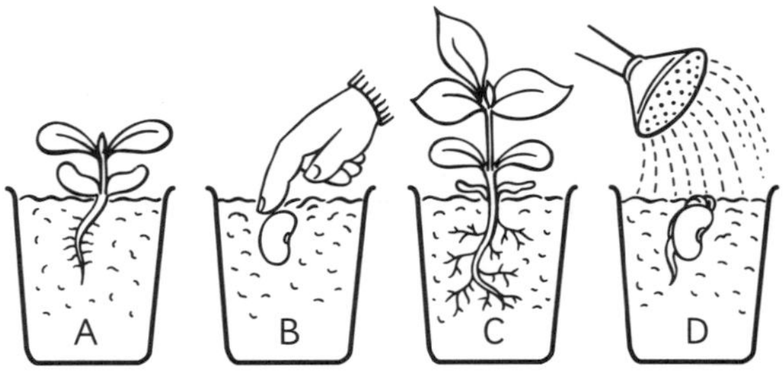

B D A C

Science investigation

How many different kinds of seeds can you find in a packet of birdseed?

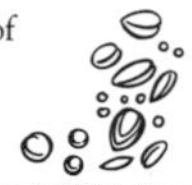

The conditions for growing seeds and the different stages of growth are introduced here. Mixed birdseed can contain sunflower and various bean seeds. When sorted, try planting them. Take care, as some seeds may be poisonous.

22

Can you find the seeds?

Background information
If you look inside fruit, you will see that most have seeds.
If you plant a seed and give it water, it will grow into a new plant.

Science activity
Find and colour in the seeds in these fruits.

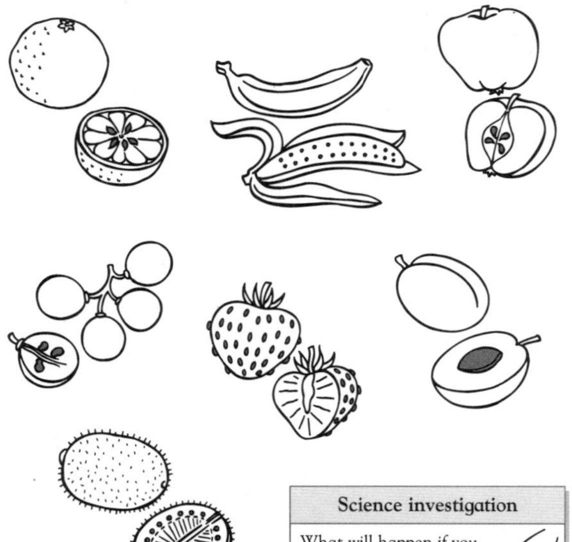

Science investigation

What will happen if you plant the seeds from an orange?

Here, your child will learn that most fruits have seeds. When planting an orange seed, use commercial potting soil or, if handling garden soil, wear rubber gloves. This prevents your child from picking up germs.

23

Where does it live?

Background information
Different animals live in different places. Some live in trees, others live in grass, on walls, or under stones and leaves. Some animals live in ponds or the sea. Others live underground.

Science activity
Draw a line from each animal to the place where you would expect to find it.

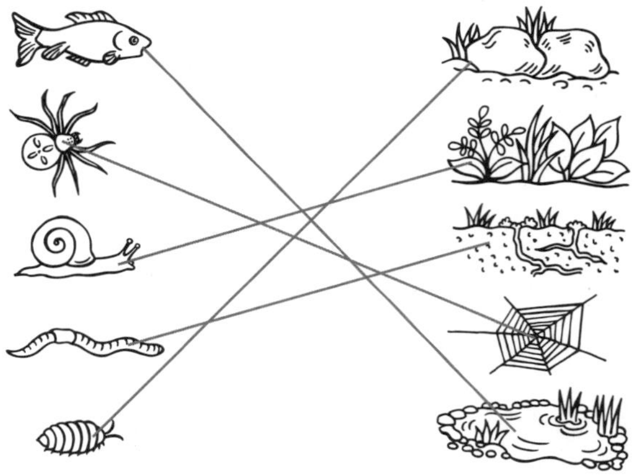

Science investigation

What sort of animals would you find living in the sea?

This page looks at how different animals live in different environments. You might like to help your child look through a picture book or CD-ROM about animals that live in the sea, for example, the *DK Eyewitness Guide Seashore*.

24 Is it tidy?

Background information
When you walk in the park, you sometimes see garbage that people have left behind. This garbage looks horrible and it can harm the animals and plants that live there.

Science activity
Look at this untidy park. Be a litter-detective and find 13 things that people should have put in the garbage can.

Science investigation

Find out where the garbage goes after the truck picks it up. What do you recycle?

This page is about the harmful effects caused by dropping litter. To extend this activity, make a list of things you can recycle in your home.

25 What is this material?

Background information
If you look around your house, you will see that different things are made from different materials. These materials include wood, metal, plastic, brick, and glass.

Science activity
What are these things made from? Draw a line from each picture to the right material.

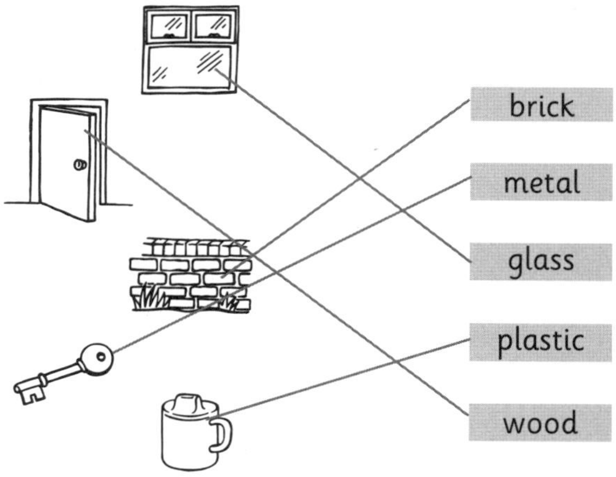

Science investigation

What things are made from paper in your house? Collect different items. Put them in order from thickest to thinnest.

This activity provides an opportunity for matching the names of common materials to their uses in the home. Encourage your child to find different types of paper and to begin to compare them using words, such as *thickest*, *thinnest*, or *thicker than*.

26 What is metal like?

Background information
Metal is a very hard material. When you hold metal, it feels cold. If you smell metal, it smells like metal. Metal things look shiny. Metal makes a tinkling sound when you drop it.

Science activity
Colour in the things that are made of metal.

Science investigation

Try holding a magnet near to different metal things. What happens?

It is important that your child learns to recognize different materials such as metal. Objects made of iron and steel are attracted to a magnet, but some metallic materials, such as aluminum and silver coins are not.

27 Does it float?

Background information
Some things float and some things do not. When you put a toy boat in water, it floats on the surface.

Science activity
Have a look at this tank of water. Draw a ring around all the things that float.

Science investigation

Does a sheet of aluminum foil float in water? Does a sponge float in water? Investigate and see if you are right.

The aluminum foil and sponge experiments help explore ideas about floating. You could also test some other household objects that are unusual in shape and vary in size to see if they float.

28

Does it change?

Background information
If you put water into a freezer, it will change into hard ice.
If you leave a popsicle in your mouth, it changes from hard ice to runny water.

Science activity
Choose and tick ✓ the correct answer to each of these questions.

What happens when you put water in the fridge?

It gets cold. ☑
It gets warm. ☐
It goes hard. ☐

What happens when you shake a bottle of sauce?

It changes colour. ☐
It does not pour. ☐
It pours easily. ☑

What happens when you put cake mixture in the oven?

It goes lumpy. ☐
It goes hard. ☑
It goes runny. ☐

What happens when you put water in a freezer?

It goes cloudy. ☐
It tastes sweeter. ☐
It goes hard. ☑

What happens when you hold chocolate in your hand?

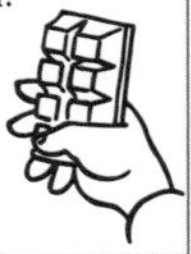

It melts. ☑
It goes hard. ☐
It tastes better. ☐

Science investigation
What changes happen when you make a Jell-O?

Every material is either a solid, a liquid, or a gas. This activity shows that solids can change into liquids and back into solids. Making Jell-O is a good example of a solid melting into a liquid, cooling and then becoming a solid again.

29

Is it light or is it dark?

Background information
When the Sun shines, it is light. At night, it is dark. You can make it light when you switch on a lamp.

Science activity
Will it be light or dark if you do these things? Put a (ring) around the correct word.

Light a candle in a dark room

(Light) or dark

Hide underneath your covers

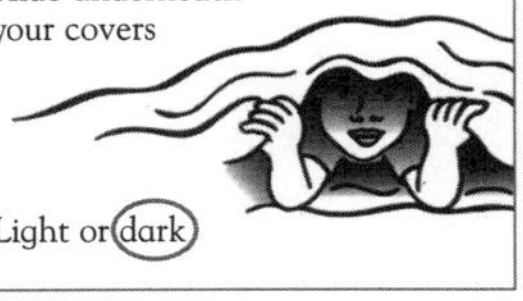

Light or (dark)

Hide inside a big box

Light or (dark)

Go right inside a cave

Light or (dark)

Turn the car headlights on at night

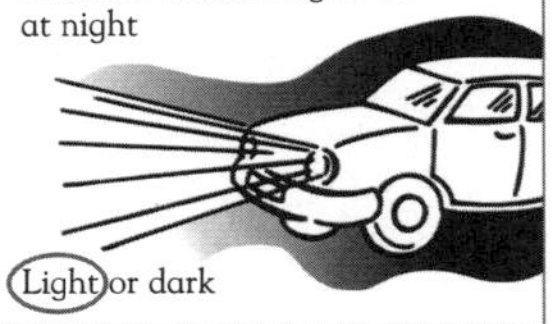

(Light) or dark

Science investigation
Can you read a book under your covers? What will happen if you use a flashlight?

On this page, the principle is that darkness is the absence of light. Dark can be made light by using some kind of illumination. Discuss the activity pictures and the potential dangers of candles and exploring places alone.

30

Where does the light come from?

Background information
It is light in the day because the Sun shines. You can make dark places light by turning on a lamp or a flashlight.

Science activity
Have a look at this picture. Draw a cross ✗ on the things that can make the room light.

Science investigation
Using a battery, some wires, and a bulb, make your own light.

Help your child identify the light sources. For this activity, one wire connects from a 1.5V battery and holder to the 1.5V bulb, and another wire connects back from the bulb to the battery. The bulb will then light up!

31

The brightest light

Background information
The Sun is a very bright source of light. You must never look directly at the Sun because the bright light can damage your eyes. Light also comes from other sources, which are not so bright. Candles, flashlights, room lights, and table lamps all give out light.

Science activity
Which of these candles gives the brightest light? Write **1** in the box by the brightest light; write **2** in the box by the next brightest; and write **3** in the box by the least bright light.

Science investigation
Draw a picture that shows three light bulbs with different brightness.

The child learns that some light sources are stronger than others. Encourage the child to distinguish between bright, brighter, and brightest. The child can use crayon colours and bulb size to illustrate different lightbulb brightness.

32 What sound does it make?

Background information
You can make *sounds* by plucking, beating, scraping, shaking, or blowing things.

Science activity
Draw a line joining each musical instrument to the word that describes how a sound is made on it.

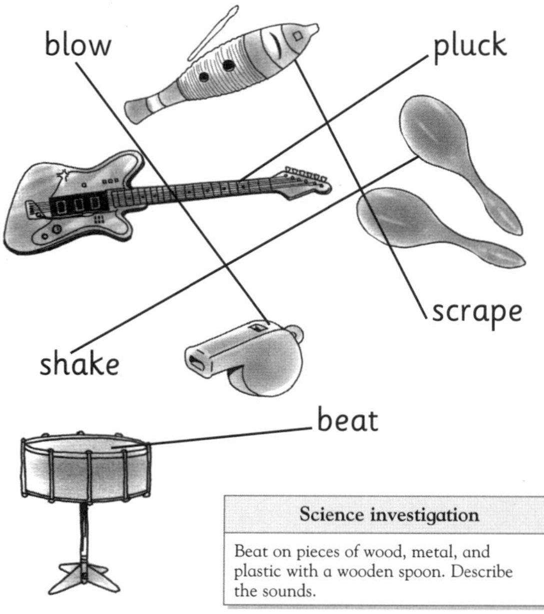

Science investigation
Beat on pieces of wood, metal, and plastic with a wooden spoon. Describe the sounds.

The child learns that different materials make different sounds, and experiments with what affects loudness. Use words such as "low-pitched" or "high-pitched" to describe sounds. If the child is taking music lessons, apply this language to his or her music.

33 How is a shadow formed?

Background information
When you shine a flashlight at a wall, the wall seems brighter. If you put your hand over the flashlight, it blocks all the light, and the wall stays dark. If you hold your hand between the flashlight and the wall, you make a shadow. The closer your hand is to the flashlight, the bigger the shadow.

Science activity
Which of the children will make the largest shadow? Circle that child's name.

Science investigation
Use a flashlight and different toys to make shadows on the wall. Make the shadows bigger and smaller.

The child learns that shadows are formed when light is blocked. Kate's shadow is bigger than the other childrens' because her hand is closer to the light source. The child should move the toy different distances from the flashlight and vice versa. Use a darkened room and bright flashlight.

34 What makes it work?

Background information
Electricity makes many things work. Some need to be plugged into a socket. Others need batteries.

Science activity
Which things need to be plugged in and which use batteries? Write ✗ for plug and ✓ for batteries.

Science investigation
Look inside some things that use batteries. Are all the batteries the same? Draw what you see.

This page highlights examples of objects using mains electricity and batteries. It is important to explain the dangers and safety rules for using electricity and plugging devices into mains.

35 Can we make it move?

Background information
You can make yourself move. You can walk slowly and you can run very fast. You can make other things move when you push or pull them.

Science activity
Think about whether you must push or pull each of these things to make them move. Draw a line to the word push or the word pull.

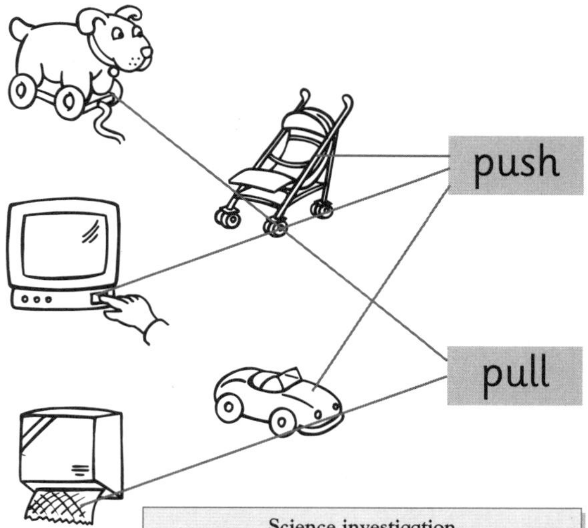

Science investigation
Make a paper plane. Do you push it or pull it to make it work? Try making it go in different directions.

Your child will learn that pushing and pulling forces make things move. You may like to show your child how to make a simple airplane out of folded paper, and explain that it needs a push to make it glide.

36

What do I look like?

Background information
When you look into a mirror, you can see yourself. You can also see yourself when you look into other shiny things.

Science activity
Draw what you would see if you looked at yourself in a shiny metal spoon.

The inside of a large spoon

The outside of a large spoon

Science investigation

What happens if you close the curtains to make the room dark, and then shine a flashlight at a mirror?

Here your child will learn about reflections. Looking into shiny surfaces produces reflections. The metal spoon will show enlarged or reduced images. This activity demonstrates how a beam of light from a flashlight is reflected around a room.

37

What is happening here?

Background information
When you put a marble on a ramp, it rolls down. When you look through clear plastic, things look different. When you look into a mirror, you can see yourself.

Science activity
Try some of these things. What happens?

What happens to a marble rolling down a ramp if you make the ramp steeper?

The steeper the ramp, the faster the marble rolls.

What happens when you look at a blue-coloured object through a red-coloured candy wrapper?

If you look at a blue object with a red sweet paper, the blue looks purplish black.

What happens if you look into two mirrors taped together at an angle?

If you look in two angled mirrors, you will see more than one reflection.

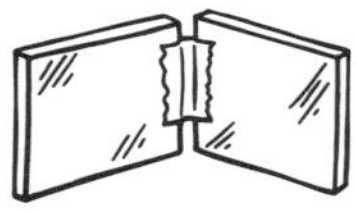

Science investigation

What do you see if you change the angle of the two mirrors?

The facts provide starting points so that your child can try to solve the three different problems using different experiments. You will find the smaller the angle between the mirrors, the more images are seen.

38

Is it alive?

Background information
You know that things are alive when you see them move by themselves. They can move without being pushed or driven, and they do not need batteries or engines.

Science activity
Draw a circle around each thing that moves by itself.

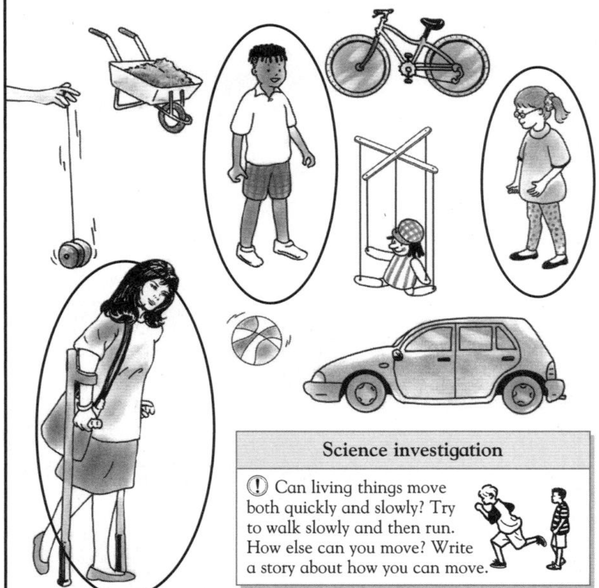

Science investigation

(!) Can living things move both quickly and slowly? Try to walk slowly and then run. How else can you move? Write a story about how you can move.

In this lesson, the child will learn that animals are alive because they can move on their own. The child should try to skip, run, hop, and walk in different ways, such as circles or zigzag motions.

39

Is it a living thing?

Background information
Living things can move, eat, and grow. Living things can make more living things. They have babies. Things that are not alive cannot do any of these things.

Science activity
Draw a circle around each living thing that is alive.

Science investigation

Name some living things in your house. Make a list.

The concept of living and non-living things is introduced. The child will often say something is alive because it moves. Discuss things that move but are not alive, such as rolling balls. Help the child develop the idea that living things can move on their own.

40 Was a non-living thing ever alive?

Background information
Living things move, feed, grow, reproduce and react. Living things that can no longer do these things are dead. Some things can never move by themselves, feed, grow, reproduce or react. These things are not alive, and they are called *non-living things*.

Science activity
Draw a circle around each thing that is non-living.

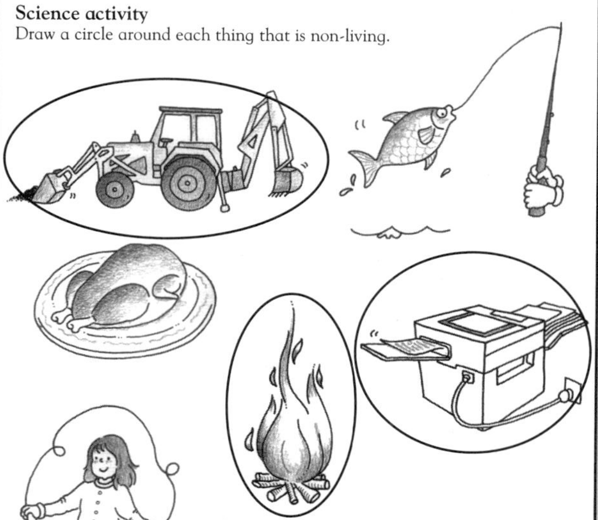

Science investigation

Learn about silk on the Internet. Where does it come from? Is it alive, non-living, or a material that comes from a living thing?

The child will learn about non-living things and things that come from living things, such as silk. Find some silk for the child to feel and compare to nylon. Silk is stronger than synthetic fabric. Encourage the child to design an experiment to test the strength of silk and nylon thread.

41 Can you spot the living things?

Background information
Animals are living things that can move from place to place by themselves. Animals are living things that eat food and grow bigger. Living things can produce babies.

Science activity
Look carefully at this picture of a farm. Colour in all the things that are alive. Find things that are not alive. Draw a circle around each one.

Science investigation

Cut out pictures or draw pictures of things that are not alive, but were made from living things.

Ask the child to colour in the objects in the farm scene. Encourage the child to think about whether the plants in the scene are alive. The child will learn that many common items come from living things, such as wood, leather, and paper.

42 What keeps things alive?

Background information
All animals need to eat food and drink water to stay alive. If animals do not eat or drink, they die. Humans are animals, too, and so need food and water to survive. Some animals eat plants and some eat animals. Humans eat both plants and animals.

Science activity
Draw a line joining each animal on the left to the food it eats.

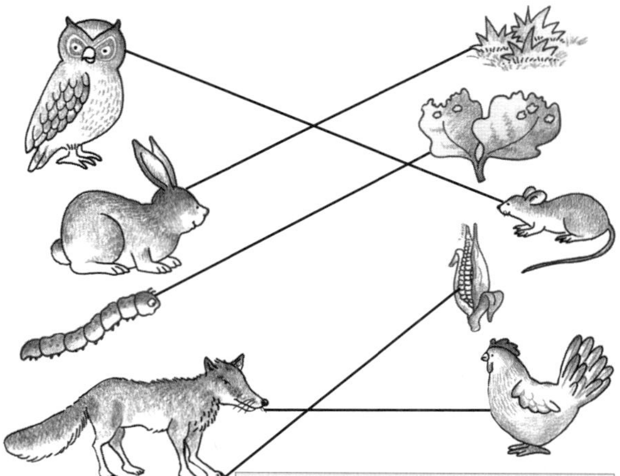

Science investigation

Make a list of all of the foods that you eat. Next to each food, write the name of the plant or animal from which it came.

Here the child is exposed to the diets of different animals. The child will learn that his or her food comes from a number of sources. Help the child identify these sources. The Internet could be very helpful.

43 Are plants living things?

Background information
When we think of living things, we often think of animals. After all, animals move by themselves, grow, feed, react, and reproduce. Although plants do not move from place to place by themselves, they do grow and reproduce. Plants are living things, too.

Science activity
Draw a line joining each whole plant to the part of it that will grow into a new plant.

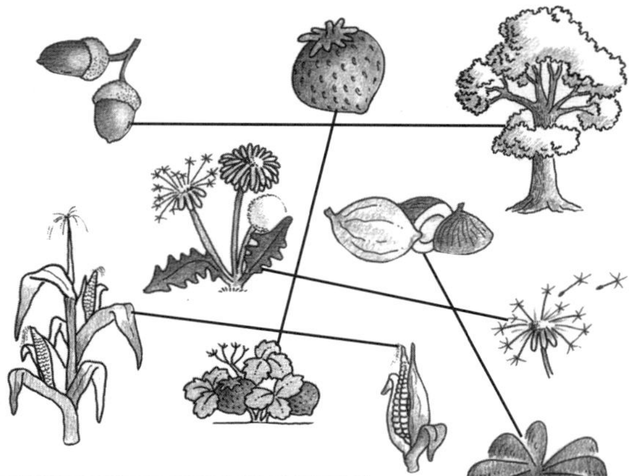

Science investigation

See if you can find an oxalis plant or prayer plant. What happens to its leaves at nighttime? What type of life activity is this? If you do not have a live plant, look in resource books or use the Internet.

Children will begin to understand that plants are alive as they view the motion of the oxalis or the prayer plant. However, growth and reproduction are the best evidence that plants are alive. Just growing plants in your home should reinforce this concept.

44 Do plants have life cycles?

Background information
Many plants produce *flowers*. Flowers make seeds. If a seed lands in soil and gets enough water, it grows into a young plant, called a *seedling*. The seedling grows into an adult plant, which produces flowers. Again, the flower makes seeds that grow into seedlings. These are stages in a plant's life cycle.

Science activity
Here is the life cycle of a dandelion. Which picture goes with which stage in the life cycle? Write **A**, **B**, or **C** in each box.

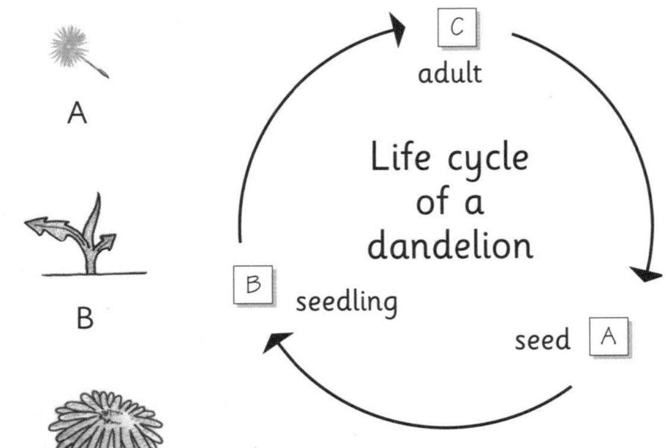

Science investigation

Draw and label the life cycle of a pumpkin.

This page focuses on plant life cycles. If possible, do the investigation in the fall when pumpkins are more readily available.

45 Are all plants the same?

Background information
There are many different types of plants. *Trees* have a woody trunk and grow very big. Some trees produce seeds in flowers while others produce seeds in cones. *Shrubs* are plants that have more than one trunk and often have flowers. Some plants are small with soft stems. They may have brightly coloured flowers; scientists call these plants *herbs*.

Science activity
Which of the plants below are herbs, which are shrubs, and which are trees? Draw a line from each plant to the correct name. What do all the plants have in common?

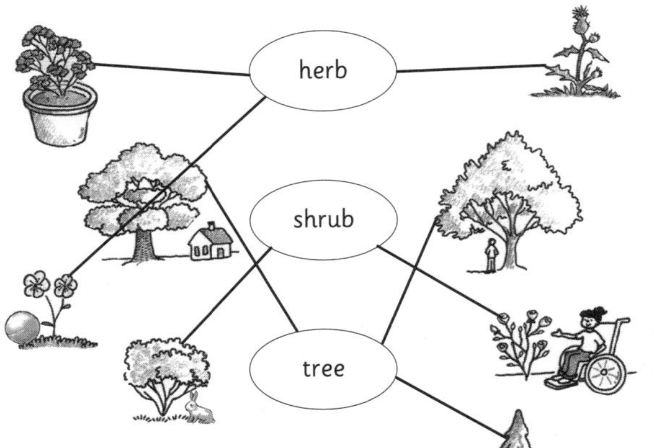

Science investigation

Take a walk in your neighbourhood. Are there more shrubs, herbs, or trees? Draw a picture of your neighbourhood.

The theme of unity and diversity in life is introduced through the study of trees, shrubs, and herbs. Ask the child how these plants differ from one another and how they are alike.

46 Where are the seeds?

Background information
Many plants produce flowers. Part of the flower becomes a fruit. Many types of fruit are good to eat. You often find seeds inside fruits. There are many types of seeds. When seeds are planted, they grow into new plants.

Science activity
These fruits have been cut in half. Find the seeds, and colour them in.

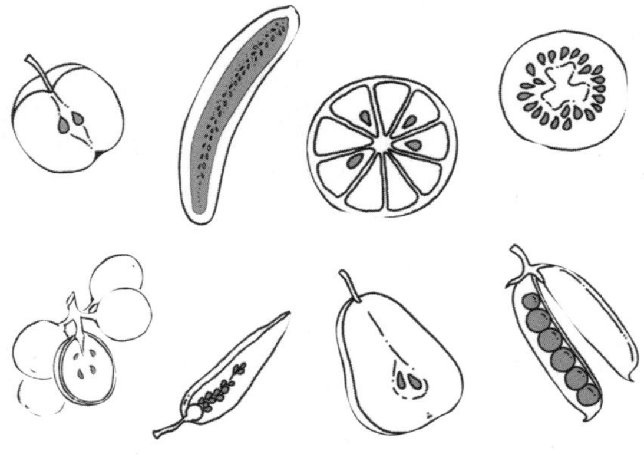

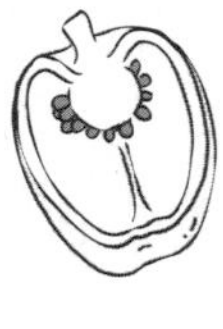

Science investigation

(!) Bean seeds grow inside of a bean pod. Soak 2–3 bean seeds overnight. Plant them in some potting soil. Draw what you see each day.

The child will see that many seeds can be found in the fruits of plants. Keep the plant in a sunny window and , if possible, continue to grow the bean plant until it produces its own beans. This will allow the child to observe the plant's complete life cycle.

47 What kind of plant is it?

Background information
Fruits and *vegetables* are plants that we eat. Fruits are made by flowers. Seeds are made by fruits. Seeds can be found inside of the fruit. Most vegetables are the leaves, stems, or roots of a plant.

Science activity
Sort these foods into vegetables and fruits. Write **F** for a fruit and **V** for a vegetable in the box beside each one.

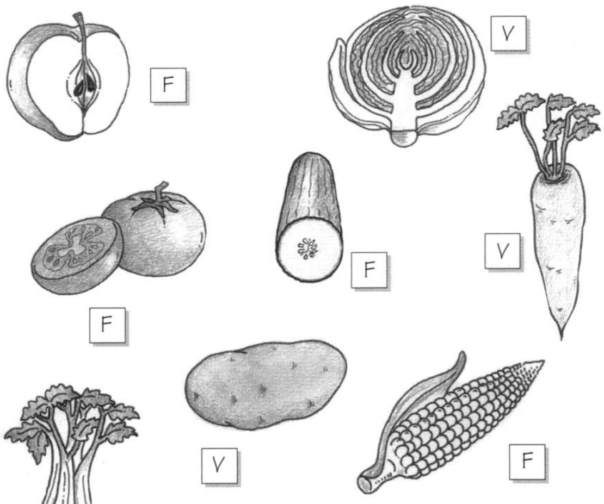

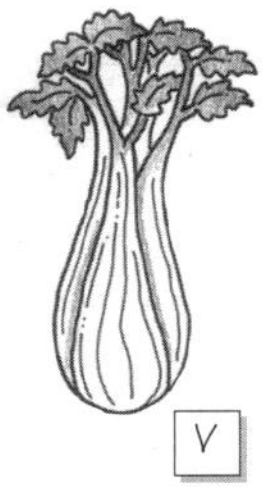

Science investigation

Draw and label what you like to put in a salad to eat.

This activity teaches how humans use plants as food, and how to group plants as vegetables or fruit. Point out that some vegetables can also be fruits, such as beans. Using resources, help children to understand more about the plant food they eat,

48

Do all living things feed?

Background information
When something eats, it must be alive. Only living things need to eat food, so they can grow and stay healthy.

Science activity
Draw a circle around each living thing that is eating food.

Science investigation

Can you eat food with either hand? Can you drink when you are upside down? Investigate.

The child will learn that living things need food. Help the child make a booklet of living things that shows what they eat. If it is possible, take the child to the pet section of the market to see what pets eat.

49

What is healthy eating?

Background information
Foods such as beans, milk, meat, and fish help you grow. These types of food have a lot of *protein.* Other foods such as pasta, bread, cereal, rice, and potatoes give you energy to work and play. They are mostly *carbohydrates.* Foods such as butter and cheese also give you energy. They are mostly *fats.* Vitamins and minerals, found in fresh fruit and vegetables, are good for you. Eating the right amount of each type of food is very important to staying healthy. Foods high in salt, sugar, and fats can make you ill if eaten frequently.

Science activity
Look at what Gus and Lakeisha are eating. Who is eating the healthy meal? Place an (✗) over the unhealthy meal. Why do you think it is unhealthy?

Science investigation

Cut out pictures of foods that make up a healthy meal. Draw and label what you ate today.

These activities help the child understand the importance of a good diet. After the child assembles a healthy meal, discuss his or her choices.

50

Which kind of food is healthy?

Background information
The food that you eat is good for you in different ways. Meat, milk, eggs, and fish all help you to grow. Bread, rice, potatoes, and fruits give you energy to run and play. Vegetables and fruits also help you to stay healthy.

Science activity
Look at this meal, and draw a line joining each type of food to one of the circles below.

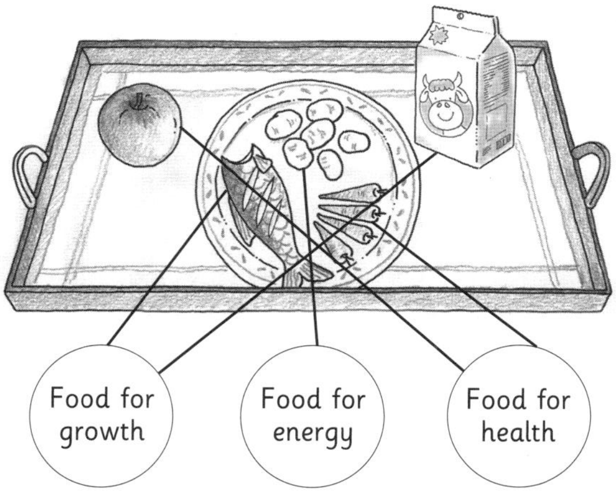

Science investigation

Do you eat healthy? Keep track of what you eat every day for a week.

Help the child with the terms protein, fat, and carbohydrate. Health Canada's food pyramid guidelines will help the child see what is needed for a healthy diet. Discuss the health implications of his or her choices.

51

How can you keep healthy?

Background information
You are a human. You need food and water to stay alive. You also need exercise, which keeps you fit. When your body is healthy, it can move easily. When you exercise hard, your body sweats. Sweat is mostly water. It helps to keep you cool.

Science activity
Place a check mark (✔) by each activity that can make you sweat a lot.

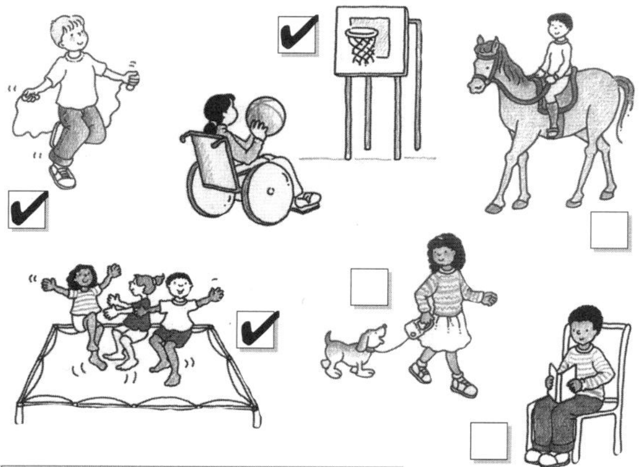

Science investigation

Make a prediction about how exercise will affect your breathing. (1) Count how many breaths you take in 60 seconds. (2) Run in place for one minute. Repeat (1). Were you correct?

In this activity the child will learn how exercise affects his or her breathing. It should be stressed that exercise is an important part of staying healthy. Take safety precautions with children who have asthma.

52 ☆1

How do we keep teeth healthy?

Background information
Some of the things that you eat and drink, such as milk, help to build strong teeth and bones. However, some small bits of food are left on and in-between your teeth when you eat. Sugary foods and drinks can harm your teeth, which may then need to be fixed by a dentist. Fruits and vegetables are healthy snacks because they contain less sugar than cookies and candy. Brushing and flossing your teeth after every meal helps keep them clean. Fluoride from water, vitamins, and toothpaste also help protect your teeth.

Science activity
Which of these foods will help keep you healthy and are better for your teeth? Colour them in.

Science investigation

Discuss what you should do to take good care of your teeth.

These activities will teach the child how to take care of his or her teeth. Stress proper diet and good hygiene habits. Discuss how to brush and floss.

53 ☆1

What are human parts?

Background information
Your body has a head, chest, tummy, legs, feet, arms, and hands.

Science activity
Draw a line from each word below to the correct part of the body.

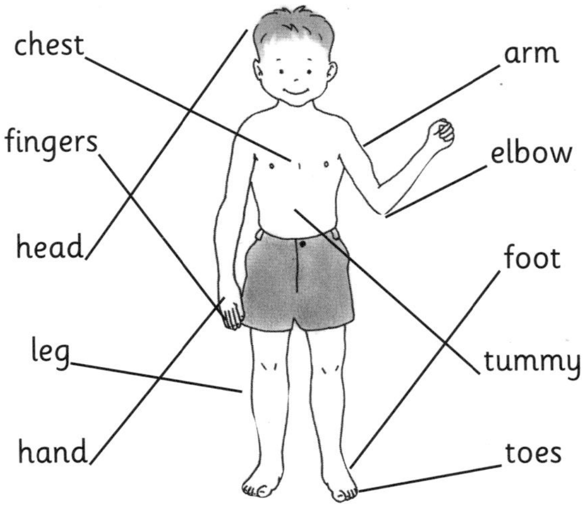

Science investigation

Rub an unsharpened pencil on the palm of your hand and then rub it on the knuckle side. Rub the pencil the same way on the top and bottom of your feet. On which side did you feel the pencil more? Record your findings.

The child learns that some areas of the body are more sensitive than others, such as the palm of the hand and the bottom of the foot. Ask the child why this is so. Explain that these areas are best suited for object manipulation and balance because they have high concentrations of nerve connections.

54 ☆1

Why do we need eyes?

Background information
Many living things have eyes. They use their eyes to see things. Many animals have two eyes.

Science activity
Draw the missing eyes on these living things. Use reference books or the Internet to help you.

Science investigation

Draw and colour the eyes of your family and friends. How are they alike and different? Find out about the eyes of animals on the Internet.

The child will learn that all eyes are for seeing, but they can come in many colours. Search together on the Internet for information about the eyes of animals, including some animals that have imitation eyes.

55 ☆1

What are noses for?

Background information
Many living things have noses, which they use to smell things. Dogs have a better sense of smell than humans.

Science activity
Guess which nose belongs to which animal. Follow the wiggly lines to see if you are right.

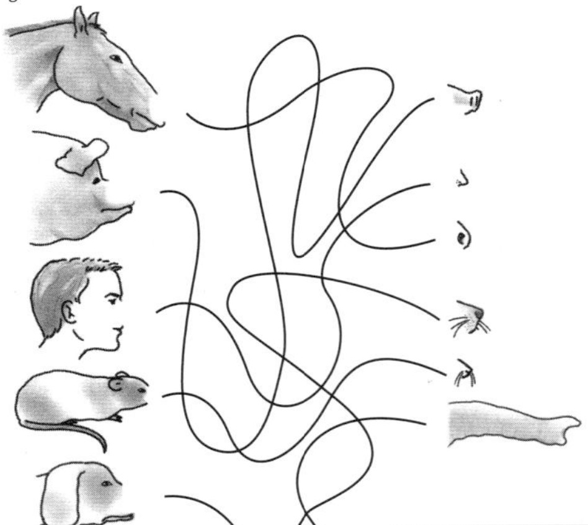

Science investigation

What can you smell? Do all things smell good? Do things that smell bad taste good? Make lists of smells and tastes that you like and do not like.

The child should be able to identify many things that smell, such as flowers and food. Things that smell bad often taste bad. Help the child with the lists.

56 What do ears do?

Background information
Many living things have ears. They use their ears to hear sounds. Dogs can hear sounds that humans cannot.

Science activity
These animals all have the wrong ears. Draw a line joining each living thing to its correct ears.

Science investigation

What types of sounds are pleasing and not pleasing? Make lists of sounds you like and sounds you don't like.

The child should be able to identify loud and soft sounds. Help him or her to identify low- and high-pitched sounds. Some very high-pitched sounds are unpleasant to hear, such as chalk scratching on a board.

57 Which sense is it?

Background information
You have senses that tell you what is happening in the world around you. Your senses give you information about sounds, light, smells, tastes, and what things feel like when touched.

Science activity
Different parts of your body sense different things. Choose words from the box below to describe what the boy and the dog in the picture are sensing. Label the parts using each word only once.

sound	light	smell	taste	touch

Science investigation

(!) Can you identify an object with your sense of touch? Place different objects in small paper bags (no sharp objects!). Ask a friend to stick his or her hand in the bag and try to identify what's inside.

The child should be able to identify his or her five senses (taste, smell, touch, hearing, and sight). Discuss with the child which objects were difficult to identify and ask what other senses may have helped in the identification.

58 How aware are you?

Background information
Your body senses and reacts to changes in the world around you. Your ears tell you about sounds; your nose tells you about smells; your tongue tells you about tastes; and your eyes tell you about light. When you touch something, your skin can feel if it is rough or smooth, and hot or cold.

Science activity
How can Sophia sense what is on the table? Draw a line joining each object to the part of her body that can sense it.

Which sense can Sophia not use?

Sophia cannot use her sense of sight.

Science investigation

(!) Have a friend blindfold you and hand you different objects. How does your sense of touch identify the objects? Did you use any other of your senses?

In these activities, the child is introduced to how living things use their senses. This activity shows children that their sense of touch can often identify an object from its shape. You may point out that blind people use touch like sighted people use their eyes.

59 Is it natural?

Background information
Some things come from nature. They are natural. Leather, for example, comes from the skin of a cow and is often used to make shoes. Some things are made from the parts of a plant. Cotton, for example, is used to make cotton shirts. Other things, such as plastics, are made in factories.

Science activity
Draw a line joining each material to the place from which it comes.

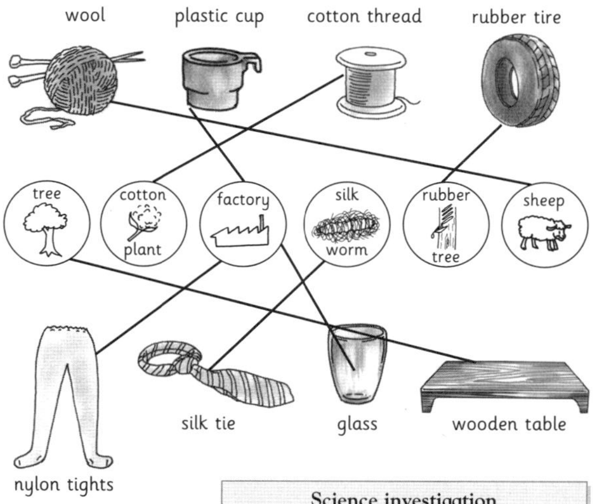

Science investigation

Make a chart of natural and factory-made things in your kitchen. Which type of thing is most common there?

The child learns to distinguish between natural and factory-made materials. This can be a difficult concept. Some children may ask if one is better than the other. The answer should be related to use, more than environmental impact, at this age.

60

What is paper made of?

Background information

Paper is made by mixing small pieces of wood with water and chemicals. Paper is used to make books, newspapers, toilet paper, tissue paper, writing paper, wrapping paper, cardboard, paper cups, and many other everyday things.

Science activity

Some types of paper are stronger than others. They can hold other objects without breaking. For example, a paper plate can hold food. Which types of paper below are strong, and which are not strong? Place a check mark (✔) in the correct box in the chart.

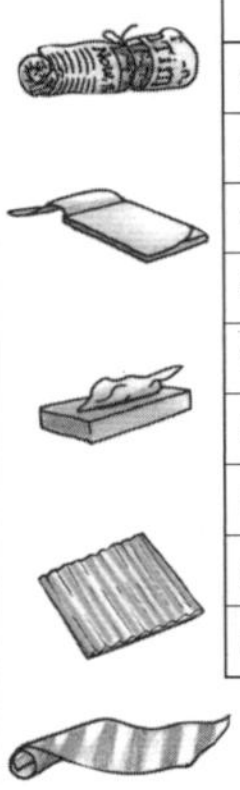

Paper	Strong	Not strong
newspaper	✔	
paper towel		✔
writing paper	✔	
tissues		✔
tissue paper		✔
toilet paper		✔
cardboard	✔	
paper cup	✔	
wrapping paper	✔	

Science investigation

Predict and test which type of paper best wipes up water. Chart what happens.

The child will design an experiment to see which paper best wipes up water. Encourage the child to explain his or her prediction. Paper towels, tissues, toilet paper, and writing paper can all be used. Ask the child which paper would do the worst job.

61

Is is made of metal?

Background information

Some objects are made of metal. Metal things look shiny. They make a ringing noise when hit. When you touch a metal object, it feels cold. Metals are used to make many things, such as the aluminum foil used to wrap food.

Science activity

Draw a line from each sentence on the left to the metal object on the right that it describes.

This metal tool used for eating feels cold to the touch.

A bag of these sharp pieces of metal used by builders has a strong metal smell.

Its loud metallic sound rings out, catching people's attention.

It is a shiny metal used to wrap food.

Science investigation

Can a magnet pull all metals? Test different metals to see which of them is attracted to a magnet.

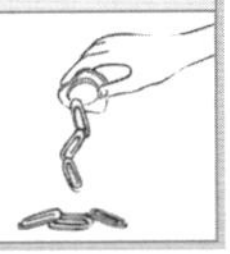

This activity introduces the child to some of the properties of metals. The child will learn that magnets contain metals, but not all metals are magnetic.

62

How do you make that sound?

Background information

You can make sounds when you beat, shake, or scrape things. You can make sounds when you pluck strings or use a bow. Blowing through a hole can also make a sound.

Science activity

Draw a circle around each instrument that makes a sound when you beat it.

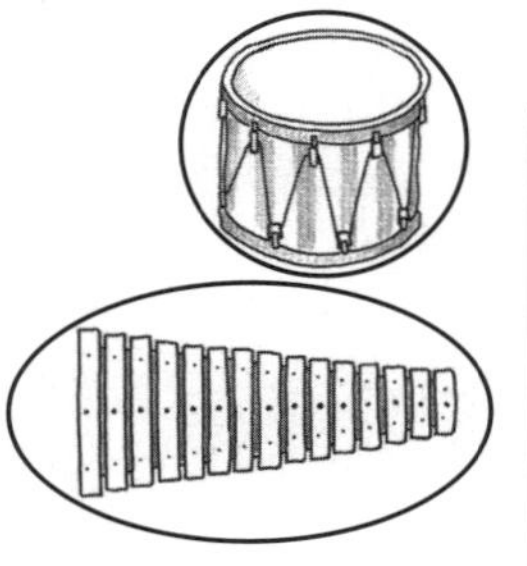

Science investigation

Blow over the neck of a bottle. What happens? Pour a small amount of water in the bottle and blow again. Add more water and repeat. Does the sound change? Explain.

The child learns how different sounds are made. Show the child how to blow across the neck of a bottle to make a sound. As an alternative, the child can tap the bottle with a spoon—the more water, the higher the pitch. A spoon-tap pitch will be lower than a blowing pitch.

63

Is it made of wood?

Background information

Some things are made of *wood*. Wood comes from trees. Many types of wood can float in water. Unlike metals, wood does not feel cold when touched. Wood can have a special smell, like the wood of cedar.

Science activity

Which things in the chart below are made of wood? Place a check mark (✔) in the correct box in the chart. The first one has been done for you.

Things	Wood	Not wood
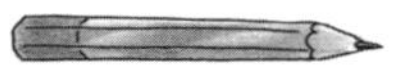	✔	
		✔
	✔	
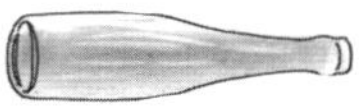		✔
	✔	

Science investigation

Place different woods in a large bowl of water. Do they all float?

The child learns that wood usually floats in water, though some woods sink. Pay attention to how high or low in the water the wood sinks. Small pieces of wood will float higher, although the salinity of the water also affects buoyancy.

64 Will it stretch?

Background information
Elastic materials stretch when you pull them. When you stop pulling, they go back to the size they were. Elastic materials also squash when you squeeze them. When you stop squeezing, they go back to their original shape.

Science activity
Annika wanted to find out how elastic bands stretched. She tied three plastic cups to elastic bands and hung the pots from a rail. Then she put three glass marbles into the first pot, four into the second, and five into the third. Here are the results of her experiment.

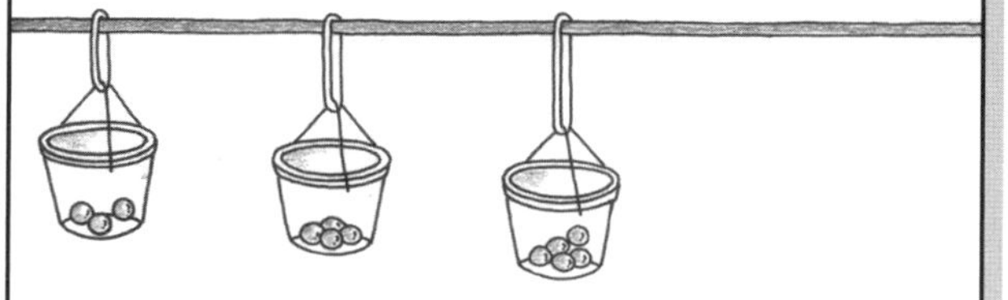

1 What happens to each elastic band as more marbles are put in the pot below it?

The more marbles you add, the more the band stretches.

2 Draw a fourth pot hanging from the rail. It should show what would happen if six marbles were put into the pot.

Science investigation

Predict what will happen when coins are added to a cup placed on a foam pillow. Test your prediction.

The foam in old pillows may have lost some elasticity. As coins are added, the foam will squash. When the weight is removed from the foam, the child will see it go back to its original shape. Ask the child to think of other elastic materials that behave like this.

65 What stretches the most?

Background information
Some materials stretch a lot when you pull them. Other materials are hard to stretch.

Science activity
Ella tested pieces of different materials to see how much they stretched. Each piece of material was the same length. She used the same heavy metal to give each material the same amount of pull. She then measured how much each one had stretched. Here are her results. Write **1** in the box under the strip that stretched to the longest length; write **2** under the strip that stretched to the next longest length; and so on.

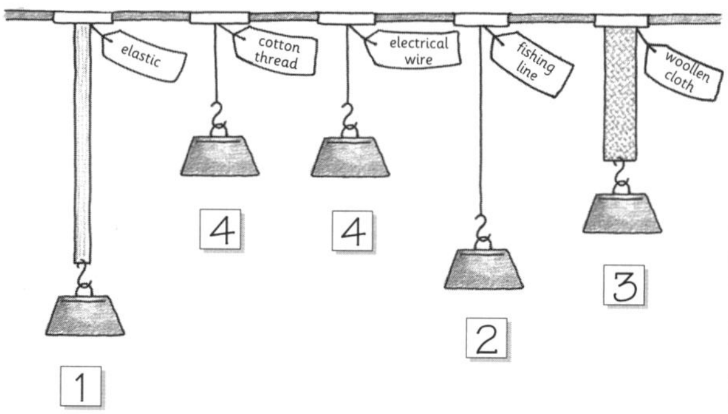

Science investigation

(!) Obtain 3-4 rubber bands of different sizes. Punch a hole near the rim of a small paper cup. Unfold a paper clip to make an "s" shape. Hook one end to the cup and the other end to a rubber band. Holding the rubber band, add pennies to the cup. Measure how much the rubber band stretches. Repeat these steps for each rubber band.

The child will learn that some materials are more elastic than others. Help the child test different rubber bands to answer questions such as, "Do thicker ones stretch more easily than thinner ones?" or "Does the size of the rubber band affect the amount of stretch?"

66 What bends the most?

Background information
Some things, such as plastic bags, bend easily. Other things, such as dinner plates, do not bend at all. The more you push or pull some things, the more they bend. Things that are not bendable may break.

Science activity
Drew is gently squeezing some cups to find out which material is the easiest to bend. Write **easy** below the cup that Drew will find the easiest to bend. Write **hard** below the cup that he will find the hardest to bend.

china

hard

plastic

....

paper

easy

Science investigation

Try to bend a stack of cards. Now try bending fewer cards. How does the number of cards affect their ability to bend?

In this activity, the child learns that things bend when a force is applied to them, and that some things bend more easily than others. Have the child make a prediction before each test is performed. Be sure that he or she wears safety glasses.

67 Is it squashy, bendy, or stretchy?

Background information
Some things you can squash; some things you can bend; some things you can stretch; and some things you can twist. When you let them go, some things go back to their original shape.

Science activity
Colour in all things that you can bend. Place a check mark (✔) by things you can squash. Place a cross (✘) by things that you can stretch, and which then go back to the shape they were before.

✔ sponge

☐ plastic comb

✔ paper ball

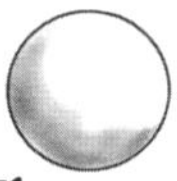

✔ rubber ball

✔ tomato

☐ plastic ruler

✘ rubber band

☐ newspaper

☐ wooden spoon

Science investigation

(!) Describe all the properties of a rubber band. Describe all the properties of clay or plasticene.

This activity shows that some materials can change their shape. Clay or plasticene also has all of the properties noted and perhaps more. For example, it can be broken apart and put back together again. Encourage the child to consider the uses of such materials.

68 Is it rough or smooth?

Background information
Some surfaces are smooth. Your hand can slide over them easily. Some surfaces feel rough. They feel bumpy when rubbed. Very rough surfaces can hurt your hand if you rub them.

Science activity
Which of these surfaces is the roughest? Which is the smoothest? Can you list these things in order of roughness? Write the roughest one first.

glass bottle

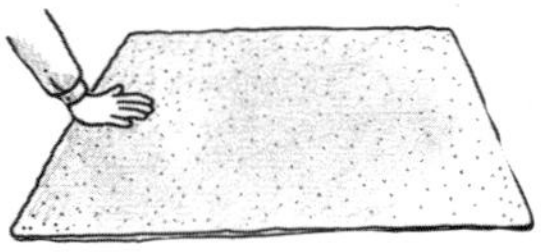
carpet

sieve

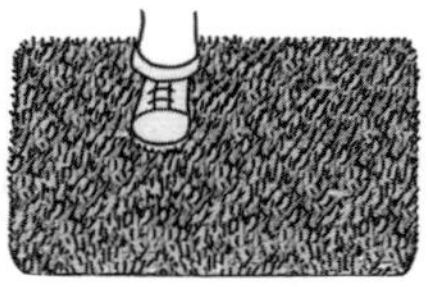
doormat

1 doormat
2 sieve
3 carpet
4 glass bottle

Science investigation
Find fabrics that feel rough or smooth. List them under each heading–rough and smooth.

Using touch to distinguish rough and smooth materials is stressed in this activity, although sight may also be helpful. Ask the child how rough things differ in appearance from smooth things. Have the child do tree bark rubbings to compare different trees' textures.

69 Is it shiny?

Background information
Metals are often shiny. If the surface of a metal is polished, you can see your reflection when you look at it. This is why metals are used to make mirrors. If you shine a flashlight onto a shiny metal surface, you can see a reflection of the light on the wall.

Science activity
Which of these spoons is made of metal? Place a check mark (✔) in the correct box.

Which of these spoons is the shiniest? Place a check mark (✔) in the correct box.

Science investigation
Make your own mirror. Wrap aluminum foil around a small piece of cardboard. Why should you smooth out the foil? Can you see things in the mirror?

The child learns that metals are shiny materials, and some are shinier than others. The child may need some help in keeping the foil smooth. Rumpled foil can be turned into a lesson; for example, making more than one mirror will show that smoother foil makes a shinier mirror.

70 What makes a thing alive?

Background information
You can tell that something is alive if it can move by itself without being pushed or pulled. Living things eat food. Feeding helps living things to grow and stay healthy. Only living things can *reproduce* (produce offspring). Living things can use their senses of taste, smell, sight, and hearing to react to the world around them.

Science activity
What is each of these living things doing that tells you it is alive? Use one of the words in the box below to complete each sentence.

reproduces	moves	feeds	reacts	grows

I know this horse is alive because it moves.

I know this bird is alive because it reproduces.

I know this boy is alive because he reacts.

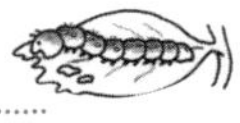
I know this caterpillar is alive because it feeds.

I know this cat is alive because it grows.

Science investigation
(!) Feed some lettuce to a land snail or a slug. How does it move?

The child will learn that living things move, eat, grow, sense things, and reproduce. A snail or slug is an excellent specimen to observe feeding, moving, and sensing things. Point out that a snail's eyes are located on the stalks of each of its antenna.

71 What kind of an animal is it?

Background information
You can recognize different animal groups by the features they have in common. For example, *mammals* have hair on their skin; *birds* have feathers; *reptiles* have scales; *amphibians* have slimy skin; and *fish* have scales and fins.

Science activity
Write which group each animal belongs to and what feature it has that tells you so.

pigeon

A pigeon is a bird.
I know because it has feathers.

lizard

A lizard is a reptile.
I know because it has scales.

cat

A cat is a mammal.
I know because it has hair.

frog

A frog is an amphibian.
I know because it has slimy skin.

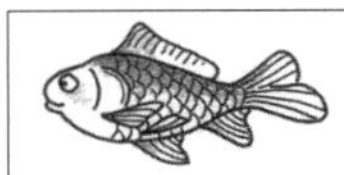
goldfish

A goldfish is a fish.
I know because it has scales and fins.

Science investigation
Learn about animal features on the Internet. Which animals are *warm-blooded*, and what does that mean?

These activities teach children how to group animals according to their features. Help the child determine which animals are warm-blooded. Make sure the child understands that human are mammals and are, therefore, warm-blooded.

72 What sort of animal is it?

Background information
If you look closely at an animal, you can count how many legs it has. This helps to tell you what sort of animal it is.

Science activity
Count how many legs each of these animals has, then find that number below and follow the wiggly line to find the animal's name.

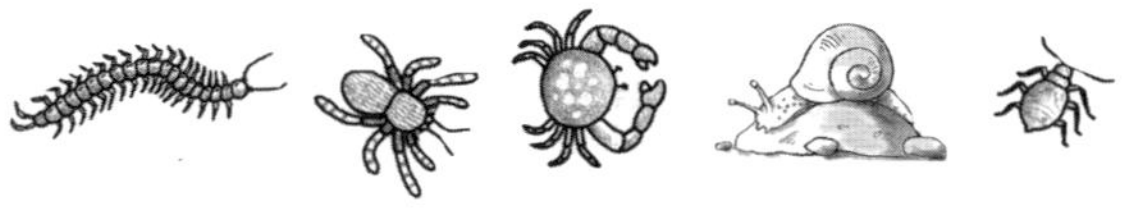

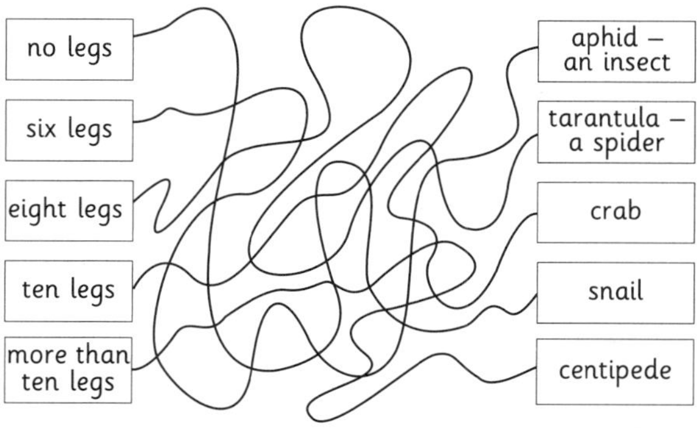

Science investigation

(!) Have an adult help you carefully collect some insects. Place them in a jar. Observe how each one moves. How many legs do insects have? Do they have wings?

The importance of observational skills in classifying organisms is illustrated in this activity. Observing an insect such as a grasshopper, beetle, or ant is an excellent way for the child to develop further these skills.

73 How does that live there?

Background information
Animals can live on land, in soil, in water, and in air. Some of these places are wet. Others are dry. Some are in bright light, others are in shade. Different animals are *adapted* to live in different kinds of places. They have certain features that are just right for where they live.

Science activity **Answers may vary**

1 Colour **orange** one part of a goldfish that helps it live in water.

2 Colour **green** one part of a frog that helps it live in water.

3 Colour **yellow** the part of a duck that helps it live in the air, and colour **blue** a part that helps it live in the water.

Science investigation

(!) If you have the opportunity, go to a garden or park and observe animals in the soil. What types of animals do you think live in the soil? Use a spoon or shovel to move some of the soil. Bring a magnifying glass. Wear gloves when you dig.

These activities teach how animals adapt to their environments with certain features that allow them to live there successfully. Ask the child if he or she could live in water all of the time. The child should wear gloves when moving the soil. Check for bee allergies.

74 Where do animals like to live?

Background information
Animals are found in many different places. Some live in gardens, some live in forests, others live in ponds, or in the ocean.

Science activity
Draw a line joining each animal to the place it lives.

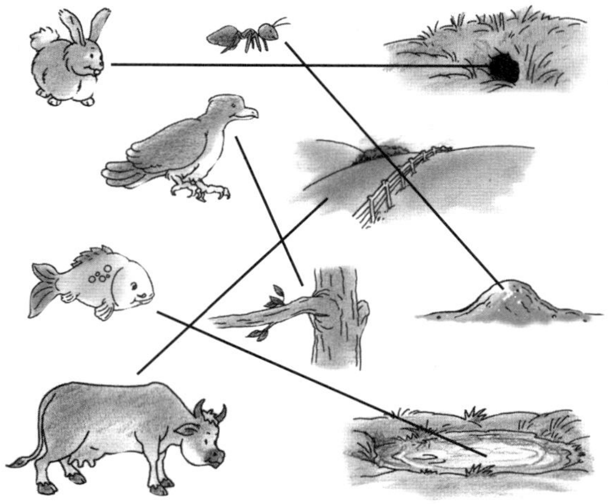

Science investigation

Dig up some soil and place it in a coffee can. Pour the soil over some newspapers and record what you see. Use a magnifying glass to see small critters. Wear plastic gloves.

The child learns that living things live in many different habitats: soil, trees, water, etc. Soil should have many small critters that can be seen with a magnifying glass. Identify them using a field guide or another resource.

75 What is a life cycle?

Background information
Adults produce *offspring*. Offspring are young animals, which will one day grow into adults themselves. These adults will then produce offspring of their own. This pattern of events is called a *life cycle*.

Science activity
Here is the life cycle of a chicken. Which picture goes with which stage in the life cycle? Write **A**, **B**, **C**, or **D** in each box.

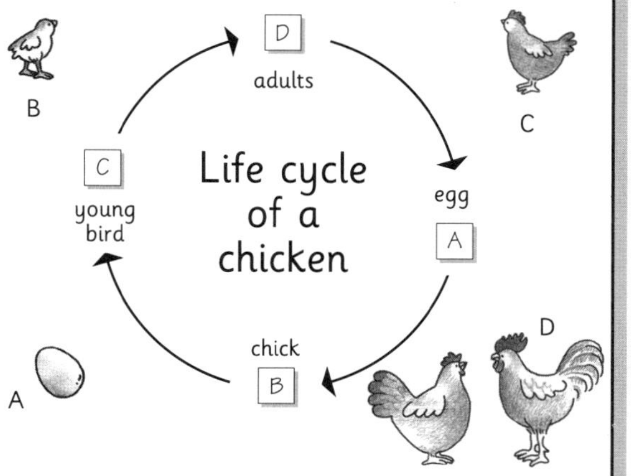

Science investigation

(!) To observe a beetle's cycle, place some mealworms in a jar with a little oatmeal and a cut-up potato. Punch holes in the jar's lid. Observe for two weeks.

These activities introduce the concept of life stages. Mealworms undergo a metamorphosis from the larva stage (mealworm) to the pupa, hatching into the adult beetle. They are sold in pet stores as amphibian food. The potato provides moisture. Lettuce could also be used.

76

What is its body like?

Background information
A human's body is covered with smooth skin. Different animals have different types of skin. Some animals have hair or fur; others have feathers. Some have scales and spines. Some have a hard shell.

Science activity
Connect each animal to the type of outer covering it has.

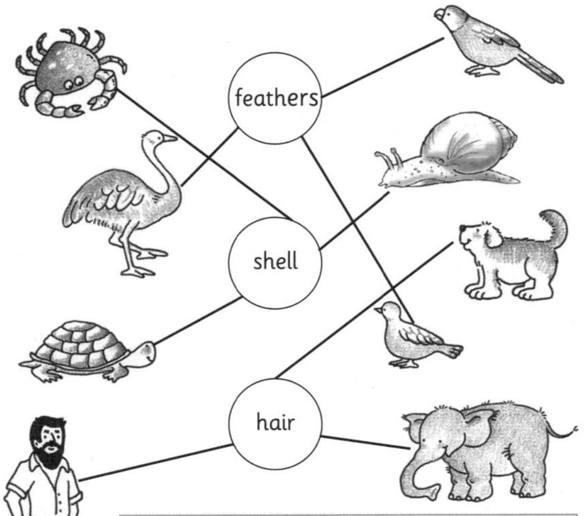

Science investigation

Cover one Styrofoam ball with yarn, stick 20 toothpicks in another, and cover a third with plastic wrap. Which covering best protects these "animals" from enemies? Explain why you think so.

The child learns that different animals have different body coverings. Help the child cover the Styrofoam balls. The child should see that the toothpick ball's covering acts as protection. Ask the child if he or she can name an animal with a prickly covering.

77

Does it move?

Background information
Living things can move by themselves. Some living things move quickly; others move slowly. Some living things run; others swim, fly, jump, or crawl.

Science activity
Draw a line joining each animal to the word describing how it moves.

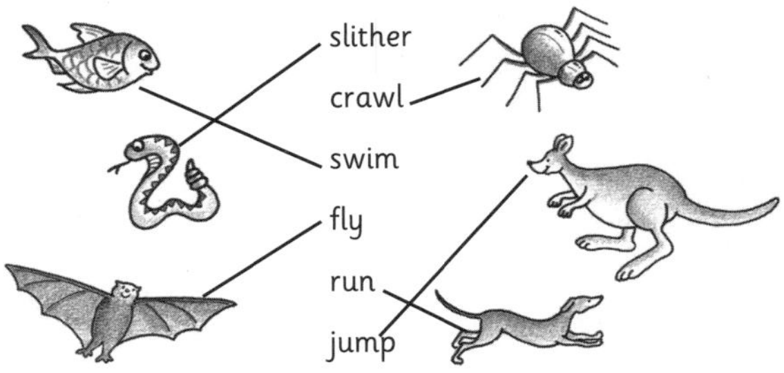

Which of these animals can move by flying?

Bats can move by flying.

Which of these animals run on four legs?

Dogs run on four legs.

Science investigation

How many different ways can people move? Record how different living things can move.

The child learns that living things move in different ways. The child sees that a person can move like many animals, but certain positions are more comfortable—such as walking on two feet instead of crawling.

78

What kind of animal is it?

Background information
There are many different types of animals. Some look alike and some look quite different from one another. One way we can group animals is by the features they have in common. For example, animals that are warm blooded, lay eggs, lack teeth, and have feathers on their body and scales on their legs belong to a group of animals called birds.

Science activity
What features do the animals in each group have in common?
What is the name of each group of animals?

Common features of group A animals:
They have fur or hair.
They feed their young on milk.

These animals are mammals.

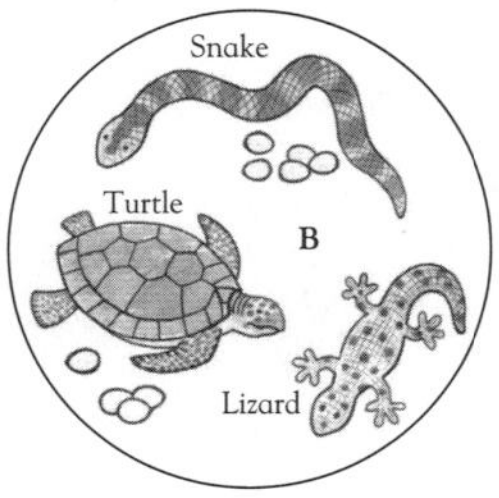

Common features of group B animals:
They have scaly skin.
They lay eggs.

These animals are reptiles.

Science investigation

Place some stuffed animals or animal toys together. Group them by their features. How many groups can you make? What features did you use? Compare your groups to the groups in the activity above.

If stuffed animals or toys are not readily available, use pictures from a magazine or newspaper. Classifying them will allow the child to appreciate the diversity in the animal kingdom, while learning how scientists classify living things.

79

What makes things go faster?

Background information
Pushes and pulls are forces that can make things move faster or slower. Pushes and pulls can also make things stop moving.

Science activity
Answer the questions about making things move faster or slower.

How can Jason make the ball roll slower?

He can make the slope less steep.

How can Amy make the ball move faster?

She can kick the ball harder.

How can Luke make the bike go slower?

He can push the pedals more slowly.

How can Anna make the ball move faster?

She can hit the ball harder with the bat.

Science investigation

Design and conduct an experiment to see how you can make a marble move quickly and slowly through a cardboard tube.

Explain that gravity is the force that pulls the marble down through the tube. The force of gravity on Earth does not change, but the marble will travel faster when the slope becomes steeper because of reduced friction from the tube.

80 Can it move in water?

Background information
Animals live in many different places. They live on land, under the ground, in the air, in ponds and lakes, and in the ocean. Animals that live in water have special parts, such as fins and flat tails, to help them move. They are *adapted* to where they live.

Science activity
Color in the animals that live in the water most of the time.

Science investigation

Set up a small aquarium for a goldfish. Carefully observe how a fish moves. With use of the Internet, learn about animals who live in water.

Ask the child how each of the animals depicted is adapted to living in water. The best way to learn about different living things is to watch them. Help the child set up a simple aquarium for a goldfish. The Internet can provide more information about animals adapted to water.

81 Is it metal, wood, or plastic?

Background information
The things around you are made from different materials, such as metal, wood, and plastic. Metals often look shiny. Their colour may have a copper, silver, or golden. Metals can bend without breaking. Wood does not feel cold to the touch and breaks when bent. Plastics can be shiny and smooth. Some plastics will break when bent and others will not. When you tap wood, metal, or plastic, they all make different types of sounds – "ching," "clunk," or "thud."

Science activity
Help Demetrius decide if these objects are made of metal, wood, or plastic. First write the words **metal**, **wood**, and **plastic** on the dotted lines. Then draw a line joining each object to the correct word.

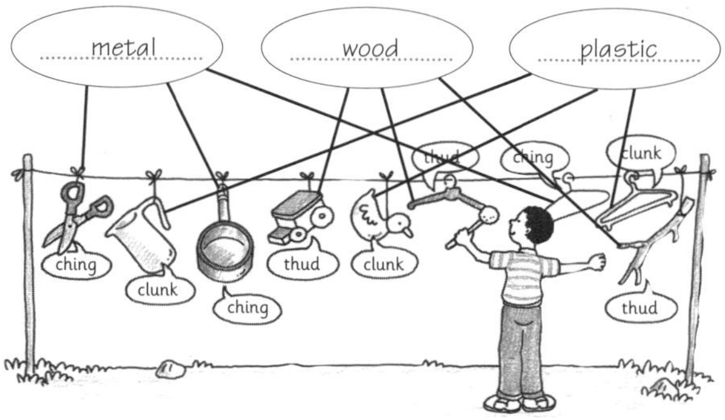

Science investigation

Feel and look at your toys. Which toys are made of plastic? Wood? Metal? Are any made of other material? Make a table to organize your findings.

This activity shows how we can use our senses to group materials. Encourage the child to tap metals, plastic, and wood while listening for their sounds. Have the child sort some of his or her toys by the main materials from which they are made.

82 Why do we use that material?

Background information
When a house is built, materials such as wood, metal, plastic, and clay are used. Each material is chosen because it does a particular job well. For example, clay is used to make bricks because baked clay is strong and does not let water through quickly.

Science activity
Draw a line joining each sentence on the left to the words on the right that describe that material's use.

Wood planks make good floors	because it lets light through.
Glass is used to glaze windows	because it does not rot.
Metal girders are used in buildings	because they're flat and smooth.
Clay is used to make roof tiles	because they're very strong.
Plastic is used for window frames	because it's waterproof.

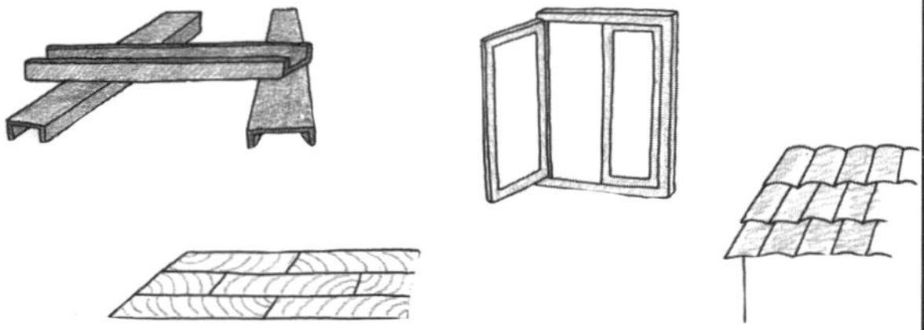

Science investigation

Design and conduct an experiment to see which type of paper is the strongest of these: newspaper, tissue paper, paper towels, or writing paper.

The child learns that materials are used according to their properties. If the child is having difficulty designing an experiment, suggest ways to test the paper's strength, such as seeing if the paper will hold a rock without breaking.

83 Can you see through it?

Background information
You can see through some materials, but not others. If you shine a flashlight on a material that is not see-through, light cannot pass through it. Some materials are not see-through, but if light is shined on one of side of them, a glow can be seen on the other side.

Science activity
Place a check mark (✔) in the correct box to show if you think each material is see-through, not see-through, or is not see-through but you can see a flashlight glow through it.

Material	See-through	Not see-through	See flashlight glow
kitchen foil		✔	
plastic cling film	✔		
tissues			✔
wooden toy		✔	
glass window	✔		
cloth handkerchief			✔
glass of water	✔		

Science investigation

Obtain different types of paper. Predict and test which ones are see-through and which ones are not see-through. Were any materials partly see-through?

The child learns that some materials are transparent, some translucent, and some opaque. The terms are not needed, just the concepts. Encourage the child to test objects other than those noted in the *Science Investigation* section.

84

Which is the best material to use?

Background information
When you make something, it is important to use materials that are right for the job. You would not make a bicycle out of tissue paper or a book out of metal. The owners of factories that make new things ask scientists to carry out tests to find the best materials to use.

Science activity
A factory owner wanted to know which fabric he should use to make swimsuits that dry quickly. He asked a scientist to do a test. She made four swimsuits of the same size from different materials, then rinsed them in water and left them to dry. Here are her results.

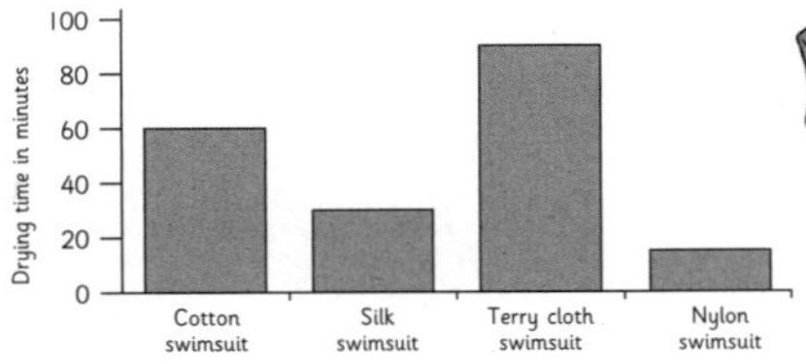

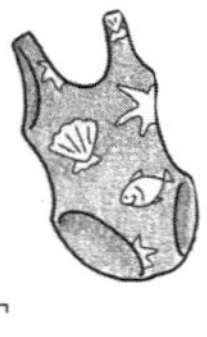

1 Which material should the factory owner choose? Nylon

2 Why is that the best choice? Nylon dries the quickest.

3 Why did the scientist make all the swimsuits the same size?

They were made the same size to make the test fair.

Science investigation

Design and conduct an experiment to see which material—cotton, paper, aluminum foil, or vinyl—would be best for making an easy-to-clean painting apron. What parts of your experiment will have to be kept the same?

This activity further reinforces how materials are used according to their properties. Interpreting information from charts is an important skill to develop. Help the child with the experiment. Use water-based paints. The child should understand that each material tested must be the same size.

85

Will it keep you dry?

Background information
Many different materials are used to build houses. Slate is a hard rock that splits easily into thin sheets. Bricks and tiles are made from clay that is baked in a kiln. Glass, made from sand, is used for windowpanes. Window frames and doors are made of wood or plastic. Building materials need to be *waterproof* to stop water coming through the roof, walls, windows, and floors.

Science activity
Jamal and Chessie stood pieces of different materials in bowls of water to find out which ones were waterproof. After a few days, they looked to see how far the water had risen up each sample. Here are the results.

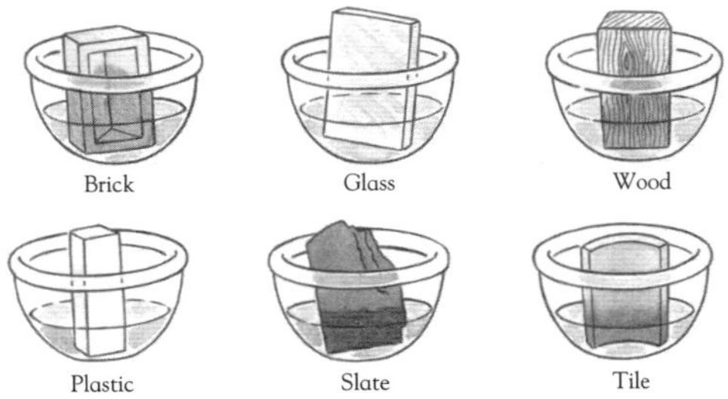

Which materials are the most waterproof? Explain. Plastic and glass, because they did not absorb any water.

Which materials are the least waterproof? Explain. Brick and wood, because they absorbed the most water.

Science investigation

Design and conduct an experiment to decide what type of fabric should be used to make a raincoat, or to see which of your family's raincoats keeps the rain off the best. Ask an adult to help you obtain samples of fabrics, or to use the family raincoats.

The fabrics that absorb the most water are least waterproof. The child might place the fabric over waterproof material and wet the fabric. Not-very-waterproof fabrics will leak onto the waterproof surface.

86

Does it float?

Background information
When you place things in water, some of them *float* and some of them *sink*. Things that float stay on top of the water. Things that sink go to the bottom of the water.

Science activity
Here are some pieces of fruit that have been placed in a bowl of water. Colour the ones that float blue and those that sink, red.

Science investigation

Gather some small objects. Predict whether they will float or sink, and then test your prediction by placing each one in a bowl of water.

The child learns that some things that feel heavy may float, while some things that feel light may sink. The explanation is too complex for this age. However, if the child has a toy boat, have him or her add pennies to the boat to see if it will eventually sink.

87

Does it change when it is hot?

Background information
Some things respond to heat by getting runny. They are *melting*, just like your ice cream cone on a sunny day. They are changing from a solid to a liquid.

Science activity
Write an **M** by the things that melt when they are put into warm places.

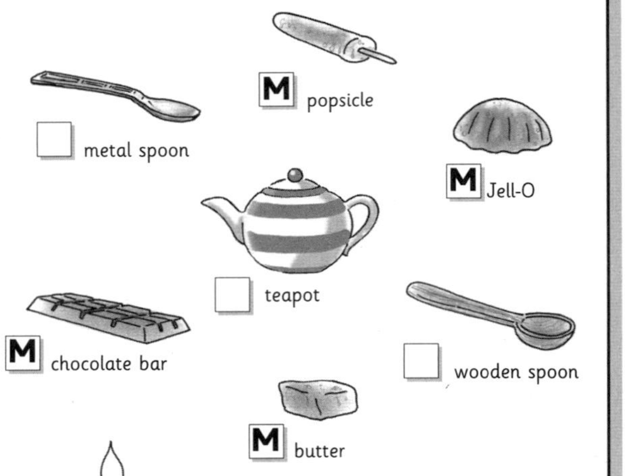

Science investigation

What happens to an ice cube placed in an empty cup in your room and left there for a while?

The child learns that some things melt when exposed to heat. The child should notice that the ice cube becomes slushy when it begins to melt. Encourage the child to use this word. It is slushy because some of the ice has melted and some has not.

88 Does it change when it is cold?

Background information
Some things change when they are cooled. For example, some things become solid in cold places. When a material *freezes*, it turns from a liquid to a solid.

Science activity
Place a check mark (✔) in the box next to the correct answer to each question. The first one is done for you.

Which one is easier to mold into things?
- ☐ Clay or plasticene kept in a cool place
- ✔ Clay or plasticene kept in a warm place

Which is easier to spread on bread?
- ☐ Butter from the fridge
- ✔ Butter left out at room temperature

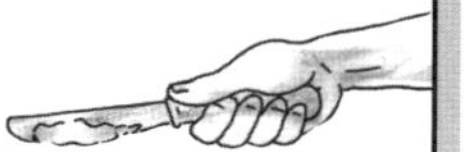

Which one feels harder?
- ☐ Water from the faucet
- ✔ Water left in the freezer overnight

Which one is easier to break?
- ✔ Chocolate just removed from the fridge
- ☐ Chocolate held in your hands for a few minutes

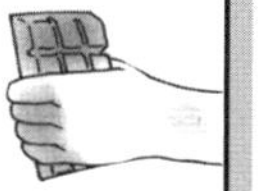

Which one is more runny?
- ☐ Ice cream from the freezer
- ✔ Ice cream you have been eating for a few minutes

Science investigation

Place some clay or plasticene in the freezer and some in the fridge. Leave some at room temperature. Compare their differences.

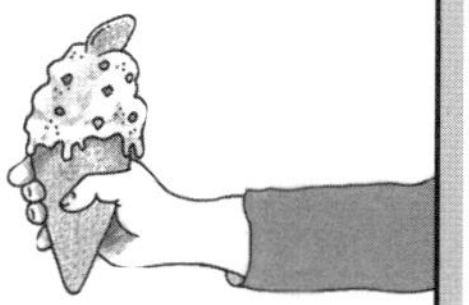

The child will learn the concept of freezing. The child will see that very cold plasticene or clay is hard to mould.

89 What cools the quickest?

Background information
When things are heated, they become hot. When heat is taken away, they cool down. Some things cool quickly, others cool more slowly.

Science activity
Jeffrey baked some cakes in a very hot oven at 180°C. He took them out of the oven and left them to cool. After ten minutes, he stuck a thermometer inside each cake. Place a check mark (✔) in the box by the cake that cooled the quickest.

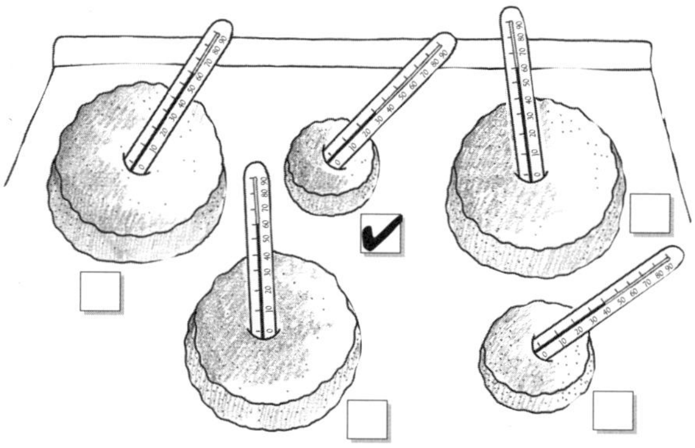

Science investigation

(!) Record the temperature of just-prepared Jell-O every 30 minutes, until it becomes solid. How does the temperature change?

The child will learn that some things cool down more quickly than others. Have the child make a data table to keep track of the Jell-O's temperature change. (This is an opportunity to learn how to take temperature.)

90 Does it change forever?

Background information
When you leave water in the freezer, it changes into ice: it changes from a liquid to a solid. When you take the ice out of the freezer, it changes back into water. When you cook an egg, it changes from being runny to being a solid. You can unfreeze the ice, but you cannot "uncook" the egg. Some changes can go back and forth, others cannot.

Science activity
Look at this kitchen. Draw a circle around each food item that changes when you heat it and then changes back again when it cools down. Place an (✘) over each food item that changes when you heat it, but does not change back when it cools down.

Science investigation

(!) Make some Jell-O with the help of an adult. Next, make some whipped cream. Can either of these foods change back into a liquid again?

The child learns about the effects of heating and cooling. Some changes are reversible, while others are not. Before preparing the food, ask the child to predict if the Jell-O or whipped cream will change back into liquid when heated. Both are reversible.

91 Will it ever change back?

Background information
When ice cream melts, you can make it hard again by cooling it in a freezer. You can make frozen ice cream soft by heating it up. These changes can be reversed (changed back). When a match burns, it changes into ash and smoke. You cannot change the ash and smoke back into a match. This change cannot be reversed.

Science activity
For each of the changes described below, draw a circle around the **H** if the change can be reversed by heating, around the **C** if the change can be reversed by cooling, and around the **N** if it can never be reversed.

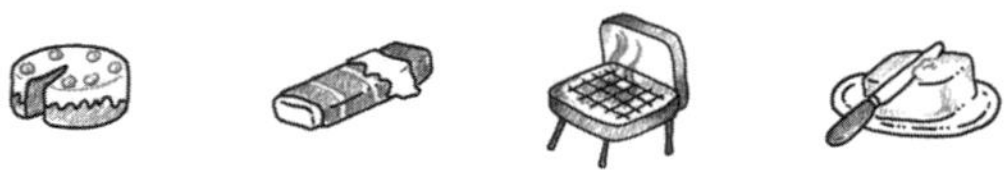

Charcoal is burned on a barbecue.	H, C or **N?**
Jell-O hardens in the refrigerator.	**H,** C, or N?
Flour, eggs, sugar, and butter are made into a cake.	H, C, or **N?**
Butter becomes soft in the dish.	H, **C,** or N?
Bread is made into toast.	H, C, or **N?**
Water turns to ice in the freezer.	**H,** C, or N?
Chocolate melts and becomes runny.	H, **C,** or N?

Science investigation

What happens to candies when placed in water? Place one candy in each of three different see-through cups and cover each with 100 ml of water. Is the reaction reversible?

The child learns that some changes are reversible and some are not. In the activity, ask the child to explain his or her choice. The changes observed are not reversible.

92 Does it make a circuit?

Background information

Bulbs, buzzers, and motors all have two ends where wires can be attached. To make them work, both ends must be connected to a battery. Batteries also have two ends, one is marked with a positive sign (+) and the other, with a negative sign (–). Always have an adult help you when you work with batteries. Here is a picture of a circuit. All the parts are joined, and the bulb is lit up.

Science activity

There is a part missing from both of these circuits, which means they do not work. Draw in the part needed to make each circuit work.

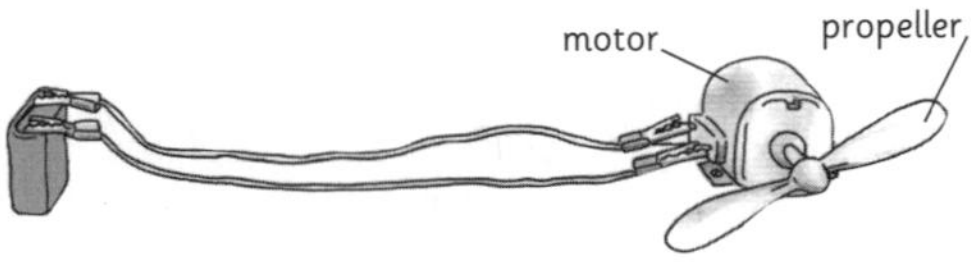

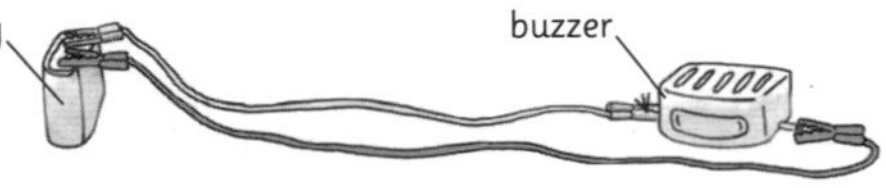

Science investigation

(!) Ask a grown-up for a 1.5 volt battery, two 1.5 volt bulbs, and three alligator wires. Connect all the parts together so that both bulbs light up.

These experiments show that a complete circuit is needed before an electrical device will work. All 1.5 volt batteries are safe, but the child may need some help in building the circuit. Use alligator clip wires, since these are easy to attach.

93 Which one moves the fastest?

Background information

A push is a *force*. A pull is also a force. Forces can make things move. They can also slow things down. Some forces can make things move fast. They can make some things move faster than others.

Science activity

Samantha is playing with a ball. Colour in the pictures where she is making the ball move fast.

Which activity makes the ball go the fastest? ....kicking..........

Science investigation

Drop marbles from different heights onto flattened clay or plasticene. What happens to the clay?

This activity illustrates how a force can squash an object. Place the clay or plasticene on newspaper. The further the marble is dropped, the deeper its impression, because the marble exerts a greater force. The child is observing Newton's Second Law of Motion.

94 Does it roll, slide, or fall?

Background information

Living things can move by themselves. Things that are not alive move in different ways. Some things fall; some things roll; some things fly; some things slide; some things bounce; and some things pour.

Science activity

Draw a line joining each picture to the word that describes how it is moving.

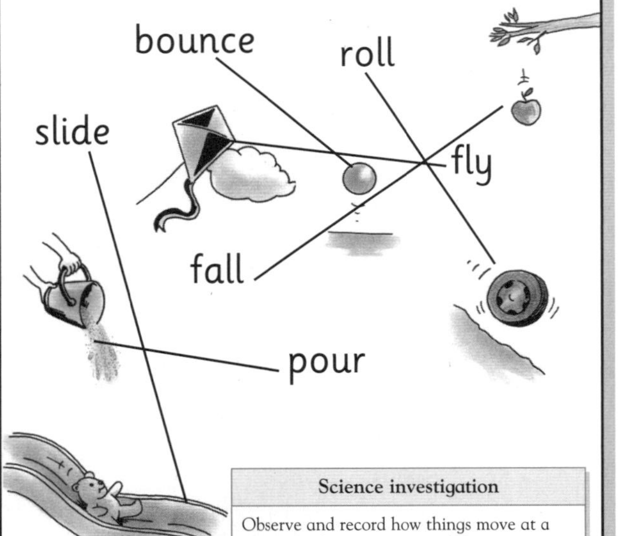

Science investigation

Observe and record how things move at a playground. Try moving in different ways. Can a ball move in some of the ways you do?

This activity lets the child observe different types of motion. The child might skip, jump, run, rock back and forth, or walk in a zigzag motion. The playground is an excellent place to observe motion. Ask the child if these motions are pushes or pulls.

95 Is it a push or a pull?

Background information

Things move when you push them and pull them. A push or a pull is a *force* that causes things to go faster or slower, or to stop. When you are very forceful (you give a hard push), you can make a toy car go fast. When you are not so forceful (soft push), the car will go slowly.

Science activity

Do these things need a push or a pull to make them move? Write push or pull under each picture.

..........pull..........

..........push..........

..........push..........

..........pull..........

..........pull..........

..........push..........

Science investigation

(!) Predict and test what you think will happen if you give a toy car a hard push and then a soft push. Try this with different-sized cars.

The child will learn that a force is a push or pull, and that hard and soft pushes affect objects differently. The child should be able to distinguish between a push and a pull.

96 How do things start and stop?

Background information
Pushes and pulls are *forces.* When you push or pull something, you can make it start or stop moving.

Science activity
Look at each picture. Is the child in each picture using a pushing force or a pulling force? Write **push** or **pull** on the first line. Does the force cause something to start or stop moving? Write **start** or **stop** on the second line.

Science investigation

Play tug-of-war with a friend. Are you pushing or pulling? Kick a soccer ball. What type of force will stop the ball?

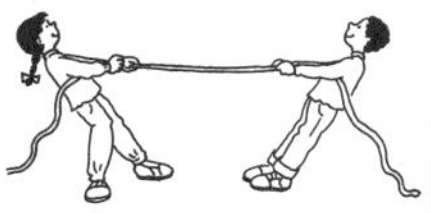

In these activities, the child learns about forces. While tug-of-war is a pulling activity, kickball is a pushing activity. Ask the child to describe other sports or playground activities that involve pushing or pulling. Make sure the child can distinguish between a push and a pull.

97 Why do things change direction?

Background information
Pushes and pulls are forces. Forces can make moving things change direction. If you blow at a table tennis ball that is rolling towards you, the ball will change direction. When you blow, your breath provides the forces to push the ball.

Science activity
Write **yes** or **no** beside each picture below to say whether or not the player is using a force that will make the ball change direction.

Science investigation

Design and conduct an experiment to see if it is easier to push a water-filled balloon or air-filled balloon into a basin of water.

The child learns that forces can also cause objects to change direction in this illustration of Newton's Third Law of Action/Reaction. The child does not need to know the law's name, but will observe that it is harder to push an air-filled balloon through water than a water-filled one.

98 What makes it work?

Background information
Many things need *electricity* to work. *Batteries* are one source of electricity. Electricity can also be obtained by plugging things into a socket in the wall. This electricity comes from wires that go into your home. Never place anything but an electrical plug into a socket or you can receive an electric shock that can kill or badly hurt you!

Science activity
Which of these things work when they are plugged into a wall socket? Which ones work with batteries? Draw a line joining each one to the correct word. The first one is done for you.

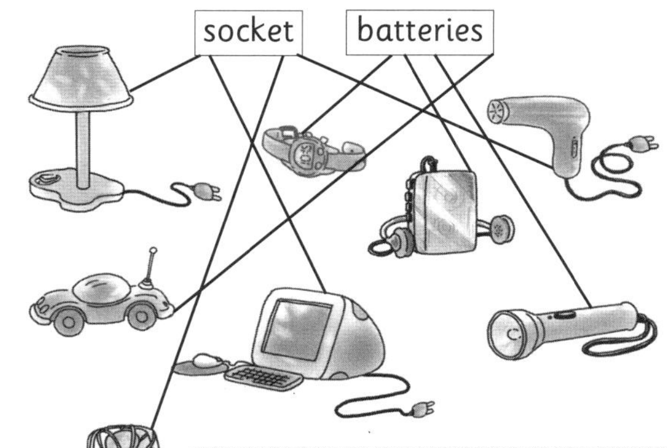

Science investigation

Cut out pictures of things that use electricity. Label each picture to show if it uses batteries or plugs into a socket.

The child learns that some things work when plugged into an outlet, while others need a battery. Make sure the child understands that some things use both. If possible, use a toy to illustrate this. Review all safety precautions when using electricity.

99 Can electricity be dangerous?

Background information
To use a hair dryer, you must first plug it into a wall socket. Electricity from the socket makes the dryer work. You must be very careful when plugging things into a socket. Never touch the metal pins at the end of a plug, and never touch anything electrical with wet hands, because you can get an electric shock. Electric shocks can hurt or even kill you. You must also be careful with electricity as it can cause fires.

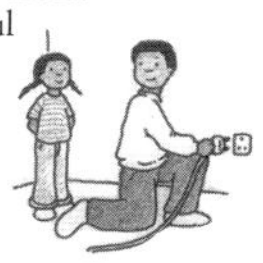

Science activity
Write **yes** or **no** to answer each of these questions.

1 Can electricity give you a shock? yes
2 Can electricity kill you? yes
3 Can electricity cause a fire? yes
4 Should you always use batteries for your experiments at home? yes
5 Should you ever play with electric plugs or wall sockets? no
6 Should you put wires into electrical wall sockets? no
7 Should you use plugs and wall sockets for experiments at home? no
8 Should you always ask an adult before plugging something into a wall socket? yes

Science investigation

How many devices are plugged into each electrical outlet in your home? Is this safe?

The focus of this activity is to teach safety when using electricity. Help the child survey the outlets at home or at school.